The Old Johnnie

1861 to 1865

Personal Reminiscences and Experiences in the Confederate Army

by
James Dinkins
An "Old Johnnie"

THE CONFEDERATE
REPRINT COMPANY
☆ ☆ ☆ ☆
WWW.CONFEDERATEREPRINT.COM

1861 to 1865
Personal Reminiscences and Experiences
in the Confederate Army
by James Dinkins

Originally Published in 1897
by The Robert Clarke Company
Cincinnati, Ohio

Reprint Edition © 2015
The Confederate Reprint Company
Post Office Box 2027
Toccoa, Georgia 30577
www.confederatereprint.com

Cover and Interior Design by
Magnolia Graphic Design
www.magnoliagrapicdesign.com

ISBN-13: 978-0692435007
ISBN-10: 069243500X

DEDICATION

To the memory of the gallant spirits who fell in defense of the Lost Cause, to their surviving comrades, and to their wives and daughters, this volume of reminiscences is affectionately inscribed by the Author.

Fair Freedom is sadly and silently weeping
O'er Martyrs who dared for her honor to die,
But myriads of Angels are sacredly keeping
Unslumbering war o'er the spot where they lie.
Rest, Comrades! the tumult of battle shall never
Break in on your dreams, nor disturb your repose;
Your valor and names shall be cherished, and even
In high honor held, 'till time's records close.

– Simmons.

PREFACE

The papers comprising this volume were begun without any plan or purpose of writing a book or of publishing them in pamphlet or any other form. They were written as opportunity permitted, in the intervals that could be spared from the duties of active business, and without any attempt at elaboration. I had entered the Confederate army when a mere lad, barely sixteen years of age; was in the first battle of the war and in very nearly the last, and when the "Bonnie Blue Flag" was furled after the surrender of Generals Lee and Johnston, I gave my parole, along with my comrades at Gainsville, Alabama, where General Dick Taylor surrendered the department in which I was then serving. I had served through the entire war, from the beginning to the end, the first half in Virginia and Maryland, and the last in Mississippi, Tennessee and Alabama. Thirty years later I was impelled, not only by the suggestions of friends, but by my own feelings and inclinations, to commence writing my reminiscences of the war and my personal experiences during the more than four years of service, more as a record for my descendants and friends to read in after years, than with any view of coming before the public in the role of author. I knew then, as I now know, that sketches, papers, reminiscences and volumes, almost *"ad infinitum,"* had been written and published, until the reading people had become wearied, if not surfeited with that class of literature. With only my original purpose in view, therefore, I continued to write as time and opportunity permitted, and now and then in order to compare recollections, submitted a paper or two to some comrade or friend in whose judgment I had confidence and upon whose memories I believed I could rely. Those to whom they were submitted were few, for I had no desire to make a public display of my simple narrative of the war, nor to give it any publicity whatever; yet, those friends and comrades who read the MSS. advised me with one accord, and some even urged me to continue and complete the sketches, and when completed, give them to the public in a volume, assuring me that they would be interesting to the public generally and specially so to all survivors of the lost cause and the descendants of those who had crossed over the river; they believed that the book would be valued by the living and the descendants of the dead who had served under Griffith, Barksdale, Forrest and Chalmers, or any where near them; and they were so flattering in their estimate, as to declare that it would be a valuable and reliable contribution to the history of the period extending from 1861 to 1865, although such a thought had never entered my mind. They believed, too, that people of the Northern States, from whose minds and hearts all bitterness had been obliterated, would read with interest truthful sketches from a Southern standpoint, of scenes and battles in which many of them had participated and of which they had heard and read.

Yielding to these opinions and representations of comrades and friends, I have endeavored to give my observations and experiences in plain and simple language, and to avoid any and every expression that might wound or offend, and in no instance to violate the laws of truth.

Reader! the result is before you; be your own judge of the merits of my work of love.

James Dinkins.

LIST OF ILLUSTRATIONS
☆ ☆ ☆ ☆

The Old Johnnie . . . . Frontispiece

"Billy" Blake 34

A Sickening Sight on the Battlefield of White Oak Swamp 46

Suddenly a Shell Exploded in Their Midst 55

Traffic on the Rappahannock 61

The Little Confederate and His Negroes 73

General James R. Chalmers 82

A Texan Makes Use of His Lasso 113

Lieutenant-General Nathan Bedford Forrest 115

Accused of Wearing a Corset 142

Captain George Dashiell 150

Lieutenant Bleecker, September, 1864 212

Major-General Edward Gary Walthall 221

We Stand Ready to Defend It 246

CONTENTS

PART I

CHAPTER ONE 17
 The Little Confederate Enters a Military School – War is Declared – Hostilities Begin, and the First Battle is Fought

CHAPTER TWO 23
 First Battle of the War Fought – Young Cadets Prove Themselves Worthy their Lineage

CHAPTER THREE 29
 The Retreat from the Peninsula – The Battle of Williamsburg

CHAPTER FOUR 33
 The Army Arrives at the Chickahominy River, and Begins to Fortify – The Battle of Seven Pines – Uncle Freeman and a Bomb-shell – Billy Blake and a Paper Collar

CHAPTER FIVE 39
 The Seven Day's Battle of Richmond – The Battle of Savage Station – The Death of General Griffith – Colonel William Barksdale Assumes Command of the Brigade – The Little Confederate Tries to Get a Pair of Shoes

CHAPTER SIX 43
 The Battles of White Oak Swamp and Malvern Hill – President Davis, General Lee and Others Meet

CHAPTER SEVEN 47
 McLaws' Division Left at Richmond – General Lee Moves Toward Washington – A Sickening Sight on the Battle Field of White Oak Swamp – McLaws Joins General Lee at Manassas – The Second Battle of Manasas – The Army Crosses the Potomac – The Surrender of Harper's Ferry

CHAPTER EIGHT 51
  The Army Recrosses the Potomac – The Battle of Sharpsburg –
  General Sims Wounded – D.H. Hill and His Nerve

CHAPTER NINE 59
  The Army Goes into Camp at Winchester – Small-Pox Breaks
  Out – The March to Fredericksburg – The Men's Clothes Freeze
  on Them – The Battle of Fredericksburg – The Enemy Capture
  Barksdale's Works, But Are Driven Back – The Washington
  Artillery Cheer Barksdale's Mississippi Brigade – Billy Blake
  and a Little Dog Frighten the People in Church

CHAPTER TEN 69
  The Men of Both Armies Become Very Friendly – The Little Confederate is Appointed First Lieutenant in the C.S. Army, and Presents
  Himself to the Secretary of War

CHAPTER ELEVEN 77
  The Little Confederate Leaves the Army of Northern Virginia,
  and Spends a Few Weeks at Home

PART II

CHAPTER TWELVE 83
  Lieutenant Bleecker Reports to General James R. Chalmers For
  Duty, and is Assigned to the Command of an Artillery Section.

CHAPTER THIRTEEN 91
  General Chalmers organizes His Forces – The Fight at
  Coldwater River – Gallant Conduct of Colonel McCulloch –
  Captain Carroll Gives McCulloch a Dining – Gallant Conduct
  of Major Grant Wilson of the Federal Army

CHAPTER FOURTEEN 99
  The Men Taught How to Jerk Beef Colonel Young and "the
  Colt" – Gallant Conduct of Major Chalmers Narrow Escape of
  General Sherman

CHAPTER FIFTEEN 107
  Fight at Moscow, Tennessee – Bright Pays His Respects to
  Carroll – A Yankee Cavalryman Kills "Uncle Steve" – A Texan
  Lassoes a Woman

CHAPTER SIXTEEN 119
   Forrest Cavalry Organized at Como, Miss. – Seventeen Men Ordered to Be Shot at Oxford The Battle of Okolona – Colonel Jeffrey Forrest Killed – A Touching Scene – The Enemy Burn Private Property

CHAPTER SEVENTEEN 127
   How the Boys Sang the Praise of the Starkville Girls – Colonel Young and Lieutenant Taylor Play a Game of Cards – The Battle of Fort Pillow – The Conduct of the Negroes – How Forrest Looked

CHAPTER EIGHTEEN 143
   A Season of Rest in the Rich Mississippi Prairies – The Battle of Brice's Cross Roads – A Jackson Girl Accuses Bleecker of Wearing a Corset – A Tournament at Egypt – General Sturges Promises to Capture Forrest – The Death of Billy Pope

CHAPTER NINETEEN 151
   General A. J. Smith Captures and Burns Oxford – Gallant Defense Made by General Chalmers – The Enemy Burn the Home of Jacob Thompson

CHAPTER TWENTY 159
   General Forrest Makes a Dash into Memphis – The Effort to Capture Generals Washburn and Hurlbut – Men Ride Into the Gavoso Hotel on Their Horses – The Plight of Federal Prisoners – How General Forrest Fed Them and His Own Men – People Thought Judgment Day Was Coming – The Negro Soldiers' Idea of Forrest

CHAPTER TWENTY-ONE 173
   General Chalmers' Movement Against Memphis – The Regiment of State Troops – Pleasant Stay at Bolivar, Tennessee – Arrival at Paris Landing – The *Undine* and *Cheeseman* Captured – First Confederate Flag Seen Afloat – Ten Million Dollars Worth of Property Destroyed in One Engagement on the Tennessee River – Official Confirmation Brilliant Work of the Artillery

CHAPTER TWENTY-TWO 195
   The Effort to Cross the Tennessee River at Perryville – Forrest and Chalmers Build Boats, Cross the River at Florence, Alabama

– Wagons and Negroes Captured – A Dutch Officer Bested by a Negro – Desperate Charge at Henryville – The Great Mistake at Spring Hill – The Battle of Franklin – Arrival at Vicinity of Nashville

CHAPTER TWENTY-THREE 213
The Battle of Nashville – Very Cold Weather – Hundreds of Men Barefooted – General Chalmers' Gallant Fight at Davidson's Landing – Colonel Rucker's Personal Fight and Capture – General Forrest Saves the Army – Recross the Tennessee River

CHAPTER TWENTY-FOUR 223
Reorganization of Forrest's Cavalry at Columbus, Miss. – The Surrender – General Forrest's Farewell Address – Tribute to General Grant

PART III.

"LAGNIAPPE" 233
King Philip – Anecdote of General Forrest – Carpet Baggers – Anecdote of Hon. Chas. Ready – "Nashville Pentincy – The Negroes

PART I

The Little Confederate

CHAPTER ONE

The Little Confederate Enters a Military School –
War is Declared – Hostilities Begin, and the
First Battle is Fought

In April, 1860, a slender and apparently delicate youth was sent by his parents from Canton, Miss., to Charlotte, N.C., where he was matriculated in the North Carolina Military Institute. He reached there very near his fifteenth birthday. It was the first time in all his life that he had been more than a day's journey from his mother. The trip required several days, which afforded him opportunity for serious thought, and by the time he was entered as a cadet he was suffering the pangs of home-sickness, which only those who have had similar experiences can appreciate, but which can not be described. The second day after reaching the institute, he was notified by an officer (a cadet) to report to Major Hill, president of the institute, for examination and assignment to class. At eleven o'clock he was told to present himself, and proceeded to do so. At the end of a large section room sat a gentleman in uniform, with spectacles resting on the extreme end of his nose, the only use he seemed to have for them. This was Major Hill. His coat was buttoned, but the first button-hole extended above the chin, the first button being covered by the second button-hole. The boy was told to salute the Major as he approached.

"Well, sir, what is your name?"
"James Bleecker."

"Well, what is your middle name?"

"I have no middle name – just James."

"Well, sir, that settled, tell me what is an equation."

The boy did not know. Then came the second question: "What is a rectangled triangle?"

He could not answer.

"Well, then, what is an hypothesis?"

He could not tell, so the Major told him to be sure to answer to his name at reveille next morning.

The boy returned to his room, having to pass several guards with bayonets fixed, walking their beats. Every thing tended to increase his loneliness and helplessness. He would fly if he could, but the guards would not let him pass out of the inclosure. The little fellow lay awake nearly all night, fearing he might not hear that drum-beat in the morning. He was down promptly, and fell in line at the foot, because he was the smallest and youngest, the roll was called, each boy answering to his name. There were several cadets with the same name. Bleecker, H.H., Bleecker, H.B., and the name Bleecker, J.J., was called but no one answered. The boy, like the others, returned to his room for study until the drum tapped for breakfast.

The front windows of the building had heavy iron bars across them, and there was no exit except by the rear stoops and stairways, to reach which all passed through a long archway. Most of the cadets had passed in ahead of the youth and just as he turned in, up went his feet, and down went his body. He was a "Newy" and was being initiated; all those behind ran over him, stumbling as they passed. It was before dawn, and dark, and the little fellow had no idea who his enemies were. He reached his room, however, badly used up, and spent the hour before breakfast brushing, and changing his clothing. The drum summoned all into line, and they were marched to the mess hall, where an officer presided at each table, and no one was allowed to take a seat without command. All sat down together and all arose together. After the ranks were broken, and all were quietly seated in their rooms, a tap was heard at the boy's door, which he opened, and there found a sergeant and two men with their guns at a carry.

The sergeant said: "I have orders to arrest you, sir, and take you to Major Hill."

"O Lord!" The boy thought his time had come. He wondered if his father had any conception of the situation. Reaching the Major's presence, that official asked: "Why were you not at roll call this morning?"

"I was there," answered the boy.

"Sergeant, did he answer to his name?"

"No, sir."

"Well, sir, why did you not answer to your name?"

"He did not call my name, sir; I was there, I declare I was there, but did not hear my name called."

"Call the roll, sergeant," ordered the Major. The sergeant began. When he reached Bleecker, J.J. —

"Stop, sir," said the Major. "Is that your name?"

"No, sir, my name is James Bleecker."

"But," said the Major, "you told me your name was 'Just James Bleecker.'"

"Yes, sir."

"Well, does not J. stand for Just?"

He had taken all these pains to play a joke, at which, however, he never smiled.

The little fellow now felt he had landed near the Inquisition, so he began to think over all the bad he had done in the past, and prepared to make amends in order to meet the dread future, which he argued was close at hand. He gave up even the faintest hope of ever seeing home again, and but for the numberless duties which he was called on to perform, might have become insane. He was careful to obey all the rules, and learn the lessons. Whenever a cadet passed a month without missing a lesson, or without receiving a demerit, he was credited with "minus a demerit," so if he should receive one, he would still be without a demerit, and thus days, and weeks, and months passed. At the end of six months the little fellow had a perfect report, and was minus six demerits.

During all this time he wrote his mother once a week, and received a letter from her each week in return. Those sweet letters from his dear mother were always full of tender expressions of love and encouragement. Mother-like, she built air castles for her boy, and looked forward to the time when he would return in vacation the next year – thought she would be so proud of him, and wondered if other mothers loved their boys as she loved hers.

The little fellow bore the separation from his mother, only because he could not do otherwise. He had but one dream in the world, and this was the hope of seeing her once more.

Winter came on with its snow, and from the mountains came covered wagons, each drawn by four large fat horses, and filled with big red apples, chestnuts and other good things. The harness of each horse contained a number of little bells, the ringing of which gave notice of the coming of all these "goodies." This was all new to the little cadet, for he had never seen much snow, and the chestnuts were entirely new to him. The jingle of those bells became sweet music to the students. When one of the wagons was allowed to enter the campus on Saturdays, it was an occasion of the greatest happiness.

The presidential election at this time was exciting the most intense interest. Mr. Lincoln was a candidate on the Republican ticket, while Stephen A. Douglas and Mr. Breckinridge were Democratic candidates, and Mr. Bell, that of the Whig party. So much excitement had taken possession of the cadets that very little advancement was made in the studies from this on. The little Mississippi cadet, who had learned the manual and field movements, found himself moving with the current. There was a division of sentiment in the school, but most of the cadets favored either Mr. Bell or one of the Democratic candidates. The election passed, and Mr. Lincoln was declared President. The secession feeling was gaining strongly, while the months passed. All kinds of stories of insurrections were circulated in the country, one having reached Major Hill that the Negroes would make an attempt to capture the arsenal at Charlotte, over which the cadets kept guard. Major Hill had served in the Mexican war, and felt no alarm, though he gave instructions for the disposition of each company in the event an attack was made. The excitement continued to increase.

Finally, the spring of 1861 found the country in a state of anxiety and uncertainty, the ultimate results of which shocked the world. The Southern States called conventions and seceded from the Federal Union and organized a separate government. War was declared, and a call for troops was made by each government. Major Hill determined to give his services to the Confederate cause and was authorized by the governor of North Carolina to raise a regiment. Men were instructed to rendezvous at Raleigh. Major Hill announced to the cadets that the school would close, and those who desired to enlist must obtain consent of their parents. The cadets, full of patriotism, and with the inspiration of youth, rushed to his banner. The little cadet from Mississippi caught the enthusiasm, but could not hope for permission to join the army. Every thing was said by the older cadets to stimulate him, and he determined to risk all and go too, and, just about a year from the time he left home, he presented a telegram to Major Hill from his father saying he could enlist. The Major was surprised at the consent, but made no further remark. (It is needless to state the message was a forgery. The little fellow gave one of the boys a gold breast pin to write it on a telegraph blank.) One hundred and ninety-two of the cadets followed to Raleigh, where they were put to work drilling the new soldiers.

Major Hill was elected Colonel; First Lieutenant C. C. Lee, who was commandant at the Institute, Lieutenant-Colonel; and Lieutenant Lane, Professor of Languages, Major of the First North Carolina regiment of six months' troops.

After spending two months in camp, drilling, the regiment was ordered to Yorktown, Va., and soon afterward fought the battle of Big Bethel. General B.F. Butler commanded the Federal forces, Colonel Hill, the Confederate, which consisted of the First North Carolina, 1,500 men, and the corps of Cadets, about 190 strong. This was the first battle of the war, though Fort Sumter had been captured some time previous. When Colonel Hill advanced on the enemy, Colonel Lee remained in the rear with the Cadets deployed, and occupying as wide a front as the regiment. The line advanced in perfect order until Butler opened fire, when it began to give way. Colonel Hill rushed to the front, calling on the men to be steady. I am satisfied it was the only time during the war he ever became excited. Lieutenant-Colonel Lee saw the situation, and called the Cadets to attention. He realized that every thing depended on their behavior, and he counted largely on the military training he had given them to overcome the shock they had received in seeing the regiment giving away. The Cadets, like the First North Carolina, never had their mettle tested before, but they had the advantage of discipline and of implicit confidence in their officers. Every thing was lost unless the Cadets could check the advancing line of the enemy. Would they do so? Who could describe the anxiety of Colonel Hill and Lieutenant-Colonel Lee in those few moments. The character of the Southern soldiers must be made within the next five minutes!

CHAPTER TWO
☆   ☆   ☆   ☆

First Battle of the War Fought – Young Cadets
Prove Themselves Worthy Their Lineage

    The feelings which occupy the mind of a soldier on the eve of battle have often been described, and doubtless all old soldiers have somewhat similar recollections of those trying occasions. There are different temperaments, and some suffer much more than others, but the rule is almost universal that a soldier is fully aware of the danger, and awaits results with a degree of doubt and uncertainty. He knows the time is too short to make amends for the past, and he finds himself in the hands of the god of battle. These few moments are awful. But the mind of a man, and that of a boy on such occasions, can hardly be compared. While the Cadets stood in skirmish line, separated five paces apart, without the support and encouragement which they would receive from elbow touch of their friends and companions, and seeing the line giving way in their front, the situation was indescribably trying. But they stood erect, eyes to the front, and all attention. There was not the slightest evidence of doubt along that line. Doctor Holmes once said: "The training of a boy begins a hundred years before his birth." The Cadets were ready to prove the statement. They were Southern youths, the representatives of a proud race of people, whose ancestors boasted a high order of manhood. These young fellows had, from the cradle, been plumed for just such an occasion, and the military training received at Charlotte, under Colonel Hill and Lieutenant-Colonel

Lee, completed the lesson, and prepared them for the emergency. The North Carolina regiment passed through our line, and the enemy was advancing. It was a moment of supreme suspense to Colonels Hill and Lee.

It has been said that "a well-bred game cock that has been without food until nearly starved, if placed in the presence of another game cock and a supply of food, would fight before he would eat." This illustrates the character of that corps of Cadets. It would be a disappointment if not allowed to advance. Colonel Lee gave the order. "Forward, Cadets! guide center! charge bayonets! double quick!" We were accustomed to his commands. His voice was musical and far reaching. It was like the blast of a bugle. The confidence, born of education and military discipline, was put to the test now, and the result confirmed the highest expectations. The boys moved forward in perfect line. There was not a waver, nor a bauble. The "minnies" began to whiz, but they only added to the determination to drive back Butler's line. The enemy was dazed by the steadiness of the Cadets, and no doubt believed that it was the advance line of reinforcements. They halted and began to fall back. The First North Carolina, seeing the enemy giving way, reformed, and rushed to the support of the Cadets. When within two hundred yards of the works, the Cadets opened fire and continued to advance. The works were taken, and the battle won.

This was an awful battle, the country thought, but it was a mere skirmish compared to what followed a few months later.

Only two Cadets were wounded, while eight or ten of the enemy were killed and a few wounded.

The battle over, the Cadets were heroes. They thought they were invincible, and longed for another opportunity to further distinguish themselves. After this battle, several weeks were spent in camp, which became very monotonous. The boys feared the war would end without giving them another chance.

During this inactivity, the little soldier from Mississippi spent much time in thinking of his mother, father, and home. He had gone into the army without the consent of his father, and without the blessings of his mother. They had no idea where he was. Many a long night he spent crying for a sight of his dear mother. He was not afraid, he did not at that time dread war, because he knew nothing of its horrors, and he had the inspiration of youth, without the wisdom of manhood, all on his side. But he was dying for a sight of his mother. He felt that if he could throw his arms about her neck, and hear her sweet voice, and gain her consent, he would be perfectly happy, but he had gone away without even telling his father, and what was worse, was living under a falsehood, which enabled him to deceive Colonel Hill. What was to be done, he could not tell. He was ashamed to let any one see him crying, and he suffered agonies. Finally the Cadets disbanded after the battle of Bull Run, and individually joined commands from their homes. The battle of Bull Run renewed the enthusiasm, and the mere thought of leaving the army would be treason and cowardice. The little fellow from Mississippi found himself with the tide, afraid to go home, and yet dying for a sight of his mother.

He enlisted in a company called the "Confederates" from his town, which was commanded by (then) Captain O.R. Singleton, and was Company "C" Eighteenth Mississippi Infantry. Soon afterwards the battle of Ball's Bluff was fought at Leesburg. Colonel Baker, a gallant Federal officer, was killed here, as was our own Colonel Burt, of the Eighteenth Mississippi; the Eighth Virginia, Thirteenth, Seventeenth, and Eighteenth Mississippi regiments constituted the Confederate forces. The Eighteenth Mississippi and the Eighth Virginia winning the honors only because they were in front. A great many were killed on both sides, and the soldiers wrote home graphic stories of the battle. The little Mississippi boy cut a lock of hair from the mane of Colonel Baker's horse, which was also killed, and sent it to his father in a letter in which he described experiences his father had never known. He remembered the stories told by him and the overseers of the hardships they endured while boys, and he compared them with his experiences. He assumed the duties of a man, and met dangers the seriousness of which he could scarcely realize. This boy had been emphatically a mother's boy, timid and absolutely dependent on his mother for every thing. What a change had taken place, it would seem, and yet he cried every night and longed to see his dear mother; but no one ever saw him cry. He was afraid they would mistake the cause. When his father learned where he was, he forthwith started to see him, taking a good stock of clothing, a bag of provisions, and his old body servant, faithful "Uncle Freeman." He reached camp late in the afternoon of a December day, 1861. He was personally the friend of all the company, and brought many of them letters and other things from their friends and families at home, but he had little time for any thing that night, except to caress his boy. Not a word was said about running away, and no regrets were expressed for the last enlistment. Every one thought the war would end before the time was out. Several days of happiness spent together, the father returned to Mississippi, where the dear mother was waiting to hear from her boy. Uncle Freeman was left to take care of "Bud" (the Negroes all called him so). There were several Negroes in the mess already, but Uncle Freeman must look after his boy, and he proved himself to be as faithful to "Bud" as he had always been to "Master." For a long time he could not reconcile himself to the scant rations the soldiers received, and spent many days exploring the country for eggs, apples, honey, and the like, which added much to the happiness of the mess.

About this time, the Twenty-first Mississippi Regiment was assigned to the brigade in place of the Eighth Virginia, and the brigade was commanded by General B.W. Griffith. The winter had far advanced; the troops were comfortable in their winter quarters, and had made many pleasant acquaintances among the good people of Leesburg. Early in the first spring month orders came to break camp, and the march was begun. The parting of the brigade from the Leesburg people was sad and touching. The citizens felt that their defenders were being taken away, and the soldiers were not forgetful of the many kindnesses they had received at their hands. Arriving at Rapidan Station, it began to snow, and soon the ground was covered several inches. The wagons were several miles behind, and the indications were strongly favorable for going to bed in the snow without tents. This condition had never before been presented to the men. Soon big log fires were built, and the snow raked away for spreading pallets, when two wagons came into camp. They contained a few tents, which were put up, and twenty men arranged to sleep in each tent. The experience was novel. The men had to edge in, and no one could turn over or change his position until all the crowd was ready. One fellow would say: "Let's turn over;" and when agreed to, all would turn at once. The soldier boy was not willing for Uncle Freeman to sleep outside, and being so persistent, the men said: "Let 'Freeman' come in;" and he did sleep at "Bud's" feet.

The command remained there only two days, and was hurried off to Richmond, and down to the Peninsula, between the York and James rivers. The position assigned Griffith's brigade was along the banks of the "Warwick," a tide river which ran across the Peninsula. Soon the entire command was busy building earth-works and filling bags with sand. Several weeks were passed here, the enemy being very active each day, trying to find out how much force the Confederates had. It got to be a daily occurrence to move up their line and skirmish for half an hour and then retire. On one of these occasions, Colonel McKinney, formerly a professor at the school, who felt some anxiety for the nerves of his regiment, stood on top of the breast-works with his arms folded, and slowly walked along, stepping from one sand-bag to another, while exposed to a deadly fire. The writer watched him, and prayed he would not be hurt, but one of the last shots fired pierced his brain, and a gallant soldier and Christian gentleman died on top of the breast-works.

The Federals would send up a balloon every day, from which they would take observations. The Confederates had no long-range guns, and shot without even a hope of reaching it. Finally, after several days, a man riding a yellow horse, hitched to a set of wheels, on which rested a long gun, shaped like a cannon, but of very small caliber, came into camp and unlimbered. He spent a few moments arranging his gun, and then looked over the ground as if to pick out a place for the balloon to fall, took aim and fired. Sure enough, the thing collapsed and came to the ground, and there it remained till destroyed. A yell went up from the Confederate side, and the man limbered up and rode off. Nothing could be learned of this man. No one seemed to know any thing about him, but he did his work, and was off. The place was called Dam No. 2, and had been guarded by a few Louisiana troops all winter, who had built comfortable houses of pine poles, and covered the dirt floors with pine straw to the depth of a foot or more. The soldiers who built the houses had been ordered to another point, and the sick and disabled men from Griffith's brigade, as well as the Negroes, were sleeping in them. Finally, a fellow who had been sick and had returned for duty was seen to pick something from his shirt and drop it in the fire. The Mississippi boy saw it and asked the man what it was. He answered by catching another and showing it. The boy's "chum" saw it and became furious; told the man to leave the mess, he was a hog; whereupon the fellow stated they were on every one, and he should not be punished on that account; but the other was obdurate and ordered him off. That afternoon, the boy and his friend concluded to go off a short distance and examine their clothes, and, much to their horror, found they were "full." They changed every thing, and, burying the suits which they had taken off, went back disgraced, in their own estimation. This, however, did not last long; – sure enough everybody had them.

After two weeks spent at Dam No. 2, the army again took up the march, this time to Richmond. Saturday night, at nine o'clock, May 9, 1862, every thing was ready to move. It had been raining several days, and the roads were very muddy and heavy. The army moved along all night, halting and starting in mud frequently waist-deep. The darkness was intense. We reached Williamsburg at sunrise. As the command passed along the street, General Joseph E. Johnston stood on the gallery of the hotel. This was the first time Griffith's brigade ever saw him. He was in command. The men were thoroughly broken down. It was probably the hardest night they had ever spent, and war in reality was on the country.

CHAPTER THREE

The Retreat From the Peninsula – The Battle of Williamsburg

The enemy followed closely our retreat, and pressed us so vigorously that General Johnston found it necessary to give battle. Griffith's brigade had been the rear guard all night. Just as this brigade passed through Williamburg, it was met by other troops, double-quicking to the rear. Soon the battle opened with fury. Battery after battery came flying through the streets, the cannoneers holding on to the limber and caisson boxes with all their strength. The broken down men and horses of an hour ago were pushing on with renewed strength and flaming eyes. The scene was exciting. Not an eye was turned to right or left. The battery horses, with their nostrils distended, every sinew in their bodies worked to full tension, went flying by. The gait was so rapid the men could scarcely retain their places on the boxes. As each battery reached position, the pieces were unlimbered, and opened fire. The time seemed an age, and yet it was but a moment. Before half the line was in position, the wounded were being brought to the rear. The battle had opened with a fury the troops had never witnessed before. Our little Confederate was standing on the roadside with his regiment, expecting every moment to hear the order, "Attention!" But the promptness of the troops sent back made it unnecessary.

The battle of Williamsburg opened while the church bells were ringing. It was Sunday, and those Christian people who had expected to offer up prayers for the preservation and success of our army, found it necessary to hunt a place of safety. The battle of Williamsburg taught the enemy a lesson, and at its conclusion we began again to march to Richmond, which continued without further trouble through the day and night. It had been raining since we left Dam No. 2, on the Warwick river. The seriously wounded were left behind. The large wagon train and the artillery cut the roads badly, and the march was through slush and mud knee deep. Frequently the heavy guns would sink in mud holes, and the men were constantly called on to put their shoulders to the wheels to lift them out. Monday morning found the dirtiest and most miserable looking body of men it is possible to imagine; but on they trudged, half dead from fatigue and loss of sleep. No unusual circumstance occurred until the following Thursday. Without a mouthful of food of any kind to eat since Monday night, the command was in bad condition and worse humor. We had reached a point where the York river on one side, and the James river on the other, ran near enough the road to allow the enemy's gun-boats to shell us from both rivers. This was very demoralizing, and was a condition which the men had not looked for. We were unaccustomed to the gun-boats, and exceedingly chary of those large shells, which filled the air with shrieks, and other wicked sounds, as well as with limbs and tree tops. The fact of their being gunboats, iron clad "critters" in the water which we could not reach, seemed a hundred times worse than we afterward found them. Fears were entertained that the enemy would land a force, and under cover of their water-craft, strike us on the flank. This was near the White House, the place where General Washington first met his wife. A few moments after, Griffith's brigade reached this point, and, while standing in mud knee deep, orders came to file out in the woods on the York river side. After reaching a slight elevation, Colonel T. W. Griffin, of the Eighteenth Mississippi Regiment, halted the command and spoke to his men. He said: "The enemy has landed a large force near the White House, and we are selected to drive them back to their boats. They outnumber us greatly, but the safety of the army requires that we whip them." He wanted the men to understand it was a desperate occasion, and if it became necessary to protect the army by sacrificing the brigade, the sacrifice would be made, but we would do our duty. He cautioned each man who had a long range gun to confine his fire to men on horseback. The enemy had instructions to pick off Confederate officers, and we would practice the same tactics. Hungry and tired, wet and sleepy, the brigade moved toward the White House. Ordinarily, such desperate conditions would have filled the men with dread; but they moved to the slaughter with no apparent fear. The shells from the gun-boats were whizzing and whirling over our heads, making havoc of the timber, but silently the men moved on. We reached a place where there had at one time been a settlement, but now only tall chimneys and beautiful trees remained, where had stood a princely home. Beyond was an open field, at the far side of which stood the enemy's line of battle. Through the foliage we could see their skirmish line. Griffith's brigade immediately formed along the skirt of woods surrounding the old settlement, and advanced a skirmish line. No more solemn occasion or more desperate conditions ever confronted a body of men than the situation at that moment. Field officers were cautioning their men, adjutants were repeating the cautions, and company officers stood behind their companies to see that every man did his full duty.

While the preliminaries were going on, the enemy retired to the river under cover of their gun-boats. Why, we never knew, but when our skirmish line advanced that of the enemy fell rapidly back. There was no battle, and, as night came on, the brigade retraced the route by which it came, and found the army far beyond the point of danger. After three days and nights without rations, and rain falling upon us continually, we went into camp near New Kent Courthouse, about five miles distant from our starting point. Soon afterward, a wagon loaded with corn was brought in, and rations of one ear to each man were distributed. Most of the men ate the corn raw, but a few tried to boil it into hominy. None, however, succeeded fully, because they would taste and taste while it was cooking until it all was gone.

Early next morning the command was called into line. The

enemy had driven in our pickets, and we expected a brush. Colonel Griffin, of the Eighteenth Mississippi, told his men: "The enemy's haversacks are filled with ham and biscuit, and if you want rations you must capture them." But the enemy consisted of a small cavalry force and did not give us the chance. That night, after halting for an hour's rest, with no hope of getting any thing to eat, Colonel Griffin told his men the orders would not permit any man to interfere with private property, yet if a cow tried to bite any man that cow must be shot. But the cow never came, and we trudged through the mud and rain all night. The following morning we drew a pint of flour each, no salt, no meat. We mixed the flour with water, wrapped it around our ram-rods, and baked it over the fire. It was the sweetest morsel our "Little Confederate" ever tasted. He was never so hungry before or since.

A few days more found the Army of Northern Virginia camped along the south bank of the Chickahominy, where in a few weeks were fought a series of the greatest battles of modern times.

CHAPTER FOUR

The Army Arrives at the Chickahominy River,
and Begins to Fortify – The Battle of Seven Pines –
Uncle Freeman and a Bomb-Shell –
Billy Blake and a Paper Collar

The Army of Northern Virginia was now on the south side of the Chickahominy, busily engaged digging ditches and throwing up breast-works. General McClellan crossed a large body of his army, and began to fortify his position on our right. General Johnston determined to prevent it, and moved General A. P. Hill's division to the attack, which brought on the battle of Seven Pines (Fair Oaks), one of the most stubbornly contested battles for the time it lasted during the war. Griffith's brigade occupied a ravine on Mrs. Price's farm, being held in reserve. The horrors of the battle could well be understood by the great number of wounded that were hurried to the rear. We expected every moment to be called on, but we did not move until after night. About ten o'clock we moved to the front, passing over the dead and wounded of both armies. Our troops had driven the enemy from its works, and far beyond, leaving its dead and wounded in our hands. Griffith's brigade stood on picket all night, amid the groans of the wounded and dying, and among thousands of the dead. We were cautioned to keep very quiet; the enemy were but a few yards from us, and would open fire if they discovered us.

Captain Bostwick, of Company "H," Eighteenth Mississippi, known as the Hamer Rifles from Yazoo county, was a very

"Billy" Blake

large and fleshy man. He owned a body-servant named Tom, who was ordinarily very faithful and generally on hand, but the surroundings just now were not congenial to any of us, to say nothing of Tom. Captain Bostwick was a fearless man, who knew no danger, but wanted to obey orders. He was hungry, and began in a low tone to call, "Tom!" *"Tom!"* "TOM!" Tom did not answer, but the Yanks did. We were lying down in a thicket of small pines, which were riddled in a few minutes. It seemed as if they had a million men, and the way we clung to the ground would have been credible to a lot of flounders. We remained quiet for an hour or so, and when daylight came the enemy had recrossed the Chickahominy. In this battle General Johnston was severely wounded. He was carried to Richmond and placed in the Ballard Hotel, where he lay between life and death for some weeks. At this time peerless Robert E. Lee was assigned to the command of the Army of Northern Virginia. Griffith's brigade was returned to the ravine on Mrs. Price's farm, through which ran the Chickahominy river, and here we remained several days watching the enemy. Each day our artillery would take position and shell the enemy, who responded in good shape. It finally reached the point when the latter would fire on a single man, who exposed himself.

During all this time our wagons and servants were far in the rear. We had not seen Uncle Freeman for two weeks, and we wondered what had become of him. He finally turned up, however, one afternoon, just as the sun was disappearing behind the woods. Uncle Freeman had been in Richmond doing odd jobs to make money, with which to buy something to eat for our mess. He reached the left of the line, and stood gazing at the Yankee camps across the river. He had a blue bucket of molasses on his head, and a sack of baker's bread and bologna sausage in his hand. Uncle Freeman had curiosity like other people, and against the advice of several men he walked up to the crown of the hill and watched the enemy. He had been there probably three minutes when about twenty guns opened on him. The shells tore up the ground and threw dirt fifty feet high. But when the dust cleared away Uncle Freeman was gone. We afterward learned he was in Richmond, nine miles away, for supper. What became of his supplies we never knew, but the circumstance made a Christian of Uncle Freeman. He held prayer-meeting every night in camp after that for a month, and would force the other Negroes in the regiment to attend. He said: "I gwine ter bless de Lord all the balance of my life, for sparing me on that occasion." Uncle Freeman, until the day of his death, would tell about how the Yankees "blowed him plumb to Richmond." We asked him what became of the molasses. He said: "Gord er mighty knows. I aynt seed em sence."

William Blake, a warm friend of the Little Confederate, was detailed by Colonel Griffin as courier for the regiment. He was called "Billy Blake," and was a pet of the entire regiment. Billy was exceedingly handsome, and up to this time managed to keep himself well dressed. He and the Little Confederate were about the same age. They were very successful foragers, and generally knew what was going on. By some means, Billy got hold of a box of paper collars, the first they ever heard of. He divided them with his friend, and they agreed when one was soiled it should be given to Uncle Freeman to wash. They each gave Uncle Freeman some soiled clothes and two paper collars, requesting him to have them ready that afternoon. Soon Uncle Freeman had the things in a kettle boiling. When he was ready to take them out, which he proceeded to do with a stick, he could not find the collars. He knew he put them in the kettle together with other things, and could not account for their absence. The two boys were sitting at the root of a large tree, watching and listening to Uncle Freeman. He said: "Hi, here! what dun 'come of dem nice white collars?" He raked the bottom of the kettle again and again, but found no collars. He then emptied the water and found a few fragments of paper. He said: "My God! dis is mighty curious. I put dem collars in that kettle sure, and I been standing here all the time." The boys heard him talking, so Billy said to him: "Uncle Freeman, hurry up! 'Bud' and I want to go." Uncle Freeman walked over to the boys with a few scraps of paper in his hand. He said: "Mars Billy, did you give me any white collars to wash?" "Yes," said Billy, "we gave you two, and we would like to have them right away; we are going to town."

Uncle Freeman was greatly troubled. He could not explain the loss, so Billy told him he must pay for them, and that each one was worth a dollar. Billy collected two dollars from him, and arranged with another friend, Jim Finley, to tell Uncle Freeman they were paper, and, of course, could not be washed. Well, now, maybe Uncle Freeman didn't rear and charge! It was a long time before Billy Blake could get any more clothes washed by Uncle Freeman. He talked about it for several weeks, saying: "Nobody but a Yankee would er made collars out of paper to 'ceive folks." Of course, the two dollars were returned to Uncle Freeman many times over.

Billy Blake was a gallant soldier, as brave as Forrest. He was desperately wounded at Gettysburg, and lay on the field a day and night without attention. He was finally picked up, but with little hope that he would recover. The Federal surgeons amputated one of his legs near the hip, but Billy still lives, and is a prominent citizen of New Orleans, where he is surrounded by a lovely family and a large circle of friends. He and the Little Confederate are still devoted friends.

Uncle Freeman was faithful and true to the last, and his honesty was unimpeachable. He was my friend as well as my servant, and, Negro though he was, I drop a sad but willing tear to his memory, and as a tribute to his loyalty.

CHAPTER FIVE

The Seven Days' Battles of Richmond – The Battle
of Savage Station – The Death of General Griffith –
Colonel William Barksdale Assumes Command
of the Brigade – The Little Confederate Tries
to Get a Pair of Shoes

      The Seven Days' battles of Richmond will be a study for future military leaders. We very often hear the expression that this or that campaign or movement was "Napoleonic," but the student of the future will find more genius in the conception of the plan of the Seven Days' battles than he will in any battle Napoleon ever fought. A writer in the Boston *Transcript* several years ago, in a commentary upon the different generals of the war, stated: "McClellan was the greatest general developed on either side, and while he was not always successful, he never suffered defeat." This statement will not be sustained by a single man who served in the "Army of the Potomac" during the Seven Days' battles. General McClellan was not only defeated at Richmond, but he was routed. Nor is this fact a disparagement of him as a great commander. On the contrary, we believe he was the only general at that time who could have saved the Union army. The attack of General Lee's army was irresistible. No troops on earth, with the arms then in use, could have withstood his charges. It has been thirty-three years since those great battles were fought, but the scenes and incidents which our Little Confederate witnessed on those occasions are as fresh in his mind as when they occurred, and his opinion of what took place then has been confirmed again and again by subsequent experience and study.

 Stonewall Jackson, with his command, was in the Shenandoah valley confronting a superior force. General Lee's plan provided that he should move with great dispatch to the rear of McClellan's right flank. The attack was made on Thursday afternoon. The enemy's right flank was doubled back on his right center, having been driven from his works at every point where an attack was made. It was hoped that Jackson would reach his rear on Friday, but he did not. On Saturday, the battle of "Gains' Mill" was fought. Griffith's brigade was held in reserve. We watched Cobb's Georgia brigade move forward through the Chickahominy swamp, under a deadly fire from what was known as the "Wild Cat Battery." This fort, from which the big guns were shelling Cobb's men, was casemated with railroad iron, which had ten to fifteen feet of earth thrown on top. In front of this, and also of the breast-works on either side, all the timber had been cut down, falling in the direction of our lines. All the small branches of the trees had bayonets stuck on them, and it was impossible for Cobb's men to make much headway, but, in spite of the obstructions, these brave Georgians pushed on. We watched them with great admiration, and saw them finally climb over the enemy's works. The enemy, however, was reinforced, and very soon drove the Georgians back, yet the gallant fellows reformed and captured the fort the second time, but were driven back again. Night closed the battle. Griffith's brigade moved forward, and remained in line of battle all night. It was understood we would renew the attack in the morning. Two men, Bateman Brown and William Howd, were detailed from Company "C" Eighteenth Mississippi regiment, with instructions to crawl as near the enemy's works as possible, and report the first movement of any attempt at retreat. We heard that in case he moved, we would attack and hold him. Brown and Howd returned about two o'clock Sunday morning with the information, but we did not advance; it was said because General Magruder, our division commander, failed to carry out his instructions. About sunrise we moved forward, and soon had possession of the enemy's works without firing a gun. As we stood in the fort and ditches, we wondered what it all meant. Suddenly the enemy's batteries, a mile off, began shelling our line. We formed on both sides of the York River Railroad. There were evidences of great confusion in the enemy's ranks. All kinds of army and camp stuff were scattered in every direction, cooking utensils, medical, commissary and quartermaster supplies, and hundreds of other things. It was intensely hot, and to prevent our men from getting water, medicines were thrown in the wells and springs.

While waiting the order to advance, a wicket shell struck the railroad section house just in our front and exploded, a piece of which we distinctly saw pass over our heads. In falling it struck General Griffith on the thigh, tearing the flesh down to his knee, while he was sitting on his horse near the fort just in our rear. He was removed to Richmond, where he died that night. His death was a great grief as well as a great loss. He was a man of much promise, and while he had already distinguished himself, would certainly have won still greater distinction had he lived.

Colonel William Barksdale, of the Thirteenth Mississippi, the senior colonel of the brigade, assumed command. We moved forward, overtook the enemy about two miles distant, and immediately brought on the battle of Savage Station (the enemy called it Peach Orchard), where only two regiments of Barksdale's brigade were engaged, the Thirteenth and Twenty-first Mississippi, but several other brigades were in it, and all together made a very hot fight. The battle was carried into the night, a terrific rain followed, and next morning the ground was covered with pools of water. Several thousand Federal soldiers lay dead and wounded on the field and in the adjacent woods. Our Little Confederate had lost his shoes in the mud of the Chickahominy bottom the day before, and asked a friend (Fort Saunders) to accompany him among the dead, and see if they could find a pair to fit. They examined several pairs, and finally Saunders said: "Here is a good pair of boots, but they are so wet I can not pull them off." He told the Little Confederate, "Hold on to one arm while I pull at the boot," and while thus engaged the Yankee's leg came off. A shell had nearly torn it off before, but we had not observed it.

When Saunders fell backward with the leg, the Little Confederate said, "I do not want any shoes," and starting away passed a man he supposed to be dead, who had a splendid haversack which the little fellow fancied he wanted. He thought it would be no harm to take the haversack, and stooped down to do so. As he pulled at it, the Yankee opened his eyes and asked for water, saying: "There is a spoon in my haversack." The Little Confederate took the spoon and gave him water from a pool near by. The man died after drinking the third spoonful. The Little Confederate did not disturb the haversack, but he kept the spoon and has it yet. It is a very large tablespoon, engraved "H. E. C.," and was manufactured by "Butler & McCarthy." He advertised it in the *Detroit Free Press* for a year, but never elicited an inquiry or response of any kind. He used the spoon through the balance of the war, but wore the end off parching corn.

On looking over the battle field, we found evidence of great confusion and defeat. The enemy threw away their guns and every thing else which would impede their flight, but the guns were nearly all bent or broken. They had placed them between two saplings as they ran and bent the barrels. Prior to this time we had very few rifles. Nothing but old muzzle-loading, smooth-bore muskets. It will, therefore, be easily understood at what disadvantage we fought at long range. The only thing we could do was to "charge 'em," and get within smooth-bore distance. Up to this time our men had driven the enemy from every point of attack. We remained in the Savage Station neighborhood Monday while the cavalry were trying to locate them. During Sunday night after the battle, "Stonewall" Jackson reached our line, but too late to cut off the enemy's retreat. Our inability to hold him in position on the Chickahominy enabled him to escape before General Jackson could arrive.

CHAPTER SIX

The Battles of White Oak Swamp and Malvern Hill –
President Davis, General Lee and Others Meet

    Monday afternoon General D.H. Hill found the enemy in what is known as White-Oak Swamp, trying to reach his gunboats on the James river. General Hill attacked him with great vigor, driving him two miles, but lost a number of his men. It was a hard fought battle, and thousands of Federal dead lay on the field. Proper credit has never been given General Hill for this engagement. He fought an army three or four times his strength, and drove them so long as daylight lasted. Barksdale's brigade reached the battlefield about eleven o'clock at night, and stood picket until morning. It was a terrible march, the night as dark as Erebus. As we worked our way through the woods we stumbled on the dead and wounded at every step, and the wounded would often cry out in their intense suffering. All night we could hear them begging for water, and occasionally one would beg to be killed and relieved of his suffering. Up to this time our Little Confederate had never seen such horrible sights, and had never been very badly frightened, but he now realized very forcibly that war was terrible, and his chances of ever seeing home again were largely against him.

    When morning came the enemy had retreated. Again our command moved slowly back into the road, leading from Richmond to "Turkey Bend" on the James river. We had nothing to eat since Saturday except green apples. The troops were tired and sleepy. Barksdale's brigade halted in the main road, and the Eighteenth Mississippi regiment stood at a point where it forks with another. There was a large oak tree in the fork, on which three sign boards were nailed. One pointing to Richmond, one to Turkey Bend, and the other to some place now forgotten. We were silently waiting and not a sound was heard. The men had no information about the enemy. President Davis, General Lee, General Jackson and a few others galloped up to the point where we were, and in a moment General Huger came up. Mr. Davis was dressed in citizen's clothes. I remember he wore a Panama hat, and I thought him the grandest looking man I had ever seen. General Lee inquired of General Huger: "Do you occupy Malvern Hill?" General Huger answered: "No, the enemy has obstructed the road by throwing large trees across it; I could not reach Malvern Hill with my artillery." General Lee remarked: "You should have done so with your infantry; move at once."

But it was too late. McClellan's army was strongly posted on Malvern Hill at the time the conversation occurred. Malvern Hill was the key to the situation, and both commanders knew it. Had General Lee's orders been carried out, the Army of the Potomac would have been prisoners the following day.

Soon after the conversation between Generals Lee and Huger, every thing was headed toward Malvern Hill. The enemy's gun-boats were shelling the woods at every point in our front. Barksdale's brigade reached a position in front of the enemy's lines, screened from view somewhat by small pine trees. We lay down and waited for the command to move forward. Large shells from the gun-boats and from land batteries, also, were tearing and literally smashing every thing in reach. The Camden Rifles, a company of the Eighteenth Mississippi, lay under a large oak tree. A ten inch shell struck it about ten feet above the ground, cutting off the entire top. This fell on the Camden Rifles, killing several men and creating a worse panic than if ten times the number had been killed by bullets. Very soon the battle opened. The enemy was massed on all sides of Malvern Hill, his artillery planted, so as to command the country for miles. One line stood above the other on the steep hill. It was a terrible occasion. Brigade after brigade was sent against his lines, and were slaughtered. It was one of the hottest battles ever fought up to that time. It was impossible to reach the top of the hill, and yet the charge was renewed time and again. Barksdale's brigade lost a great many good men. Captain E.G. Henry, of Company "C," Eighteenth Mississippi, was wounded in the leg, about one hundred yards from the enemy's lines, and bled to death before assistance reached him. He was a patriot in the highest sense, a man who regarded duty above all other considerations. A great many others were killed, but I remember the universal sorrow at the death of Green B. Crane, a young man of faultless character. He graduated at the University of Mississippi at the breaking out of the war, and gave promise of a brilliant future. He was brave as Cæsar, determined as Jackson, and gentle as Ruth. He was liberal, chivalrous and companionable. What more could be said of him? The Little Confederate and Green Crane were schoolmates, and he remembers him with deep and tender affection. The horrors of the battle of Malvern Hill can never be known, and hardly even imagined by those who were not there. While the enemy retreated during the night, our army was badly crippled, but remained on the field. We had retained our position, but at tremendous sacrifice. What the result would have been had General Lee's orders been carried out must forever remain unknown.

A Sickening Sight on the Battlefield of White Oak Swamp

CHAPTER SEVEN

McLaws' Division Left at Richmond – General Lee
Moves Toward Washington – A Sickening Sight on the
Battle Field of White Oak Swamp – McLaws Joins
General Lee at Manassas – The Second Battle of
Manassas – The Army Crosses the Potomac –
The Surrender at Harper's Ferry

After the enemy had retreated, the Army of Northern Virginia went into camp along the James river, and Barksdale's brigade was located at Camp Holly, General Washington's old camp. A fine field of corn in roasting-ear furnished rations for the army for several days. Eight or ten ears at a meal was an average dinner for a man. McClelland was superseded in command of the Army of the Potomac by General Pope. This occurred a few weeks after the battle of Richmond. General Lee, with most of his army, moved in the direction of Manassas, and was met by General Pope, and here was fought the second battle of Manassas, the enemy occupying the position the Confederate army occupied at the first battle. McLaws' division of Longstreet's corps was left behind to defend Richmond, and the enemy also left a force to keep McLaws busy. About two weeks after the battle of Malvern Hill the enemy made a demonstration which was promptly met by General McLaws. In passing through a part of White Oak battle field, we came to a plank fence about a mile long. This fence passed through timber, and here we saw a most harrowing sight. Five or six hundred dead Yankees were hanging across the fence, killed as they were getting over. The buzzards had torn their clothing nearly off and stripped the flesh from their bones. They were scarcely any thing but bones and rags when we saw them. The skulls with hair on them looked horrible. These poor men were killed in the Monday night – General D. H. Hill's – fight. The Little Confederate was beginning to grow case hardened. Dead men were so common, little notice was taken of them. Soon after this circumstance McLaws' division, of which Barksdale's brigade formed a part, hurried to Richmond, thence to Hanover Junction. We found tents already stretched, and occupied them about two hours, when a terrible storm came up which blew down every thing. We reached Hanover Junction by rail, but "hoofed it" the balance of the way to Warrenton, near Manassas, where we found thousands and thousands of dead Federals. One might have walked five miles on dead men. It was two days after the second battle of Manassas. The weather was fearfully hot, and decomposition had set in. The bodies were all swollen, and presented the appearance of men weighing three hundred pounds. The enemy's ambulance corps was busy burying the dead under flag of truce. The Little Confederate saw a man looking into the mouths of the dead Yankees. They were wide open. When the man found a tooth plugged with gold, he knocked it out with his bayonet. We saw him afterward with a pocket full of teeth.

There was a regiment of "Bucktail Zouaves," I think, One Hundred and Eighth New York, about eight hundred strong. Nearly all of them were killed. General Gregg's Texas brigade lay in the sedge grass several hundred yards in advance of a battery of the Richmond Howitzers, which was playing havoc on the enemy's lines. The Bucktails, we supposed, were ordered to take the battery. They were dressed in red pants and blue jackets. Every man had a buck's tail in his hat. They moved at double quick on the battery, unconscious of Gregg's men in the sedge. When within fifty yards, the Texans took deliberate aim and killed almost every man. Over seven hundred Bucktails lay in line. It was awful! They were good soldiers, and it was a pity, but it was war. The Little Confederate found a buck's tail and wore it in his hat, until some old ragged rebel appropriated it without so much as as saying "Boo." We proceeded from here to Leesburg, Va., where Barksdale's brigade had spent the winter of 1861 and 1862. The people were delighted to see us, and filled our haversacks with "grub." It was difficult to get Barksdale's brigade to move. Beautiful women, married and single, hung around them, recalling the happy associations of the preceding winter.

Just before the Seven Days' battle Uncle Freeman was taken sick, and the Little Confederate wrote his father to send "Matt" to take his place, it being the intention to send Uncle Freeman home. Matt was sent at once, and reached the command at Leesburg, but by that time Uncle Freeman had gotten well, and was not willing to leave "Master's boy," so both continued with us as long as the Little Confederate remained with the Army of Northern Virginia. Matt was a great favorite with his master's family, and when he left home promised to look well after his young master. He reached camp with two good suits of clothes and shoes for the Little Confederate. He had, also, a number of letters for different members of Company "C." We listened to Matt talk nearly all night. The last thing before going to sleep he said to his young master: "When you get tired, you get on Matt's back. He carried you before this, and he can carry you now." But the Little Confederate said: "Matt, you keep up, I will be there when we stop."

The army crossed the Potomac river at the "Point of Rocks," not far above Leesburg, and marched to Frederick City, Maryland. We remained here a few days, when McLaws' division moved toward Hagerstown, thence to Harper's Ferry, where the enemy had a force of twenty-eight thousand men. Barksdale's brigade was put in front, and reached Maryland Heights, opposite Harper's Ferry. The enemy had no idea of allowing us to climb the heights, and opened on our column with his big guns. We were four days storming the heights. Whatever ground we gained during the day we pulled our guns over at night. The mountain was very steep. We carried up the wheels and axles one at a time, and a hundred or more men would pull the guns up with ropes. By day we would have our guns in position, and open on the enemy as soon as it was light. We would often reach a large boulder which it was necessary to pass. The enemy's big shells would strike them and scatter small pieces of rock in all directions. We advanced under heavy fire, but very slowly. Nothing to eat, and no water, though the Potomac was within two miles. We finally reached the summit, having driven the enemy into Harper's Ferry. We were nearly starved. We scrambled over the bread crusts, onion peels, and meat skins that the enemy had thrown away. Stonewall Jackson had Harper's Ferry surrounded on both sides of the river. About midnight, after capturing Maryland Heights, Barksdale's brigade was hurried down the valley to meet a column of the enemy coming to the relief of Harper's Ferry. We double-quicked about five miles, and by dawn formed a line along a ridge. We could plainly see the enemy's camp, and his guns stacked. We expected an engagement every minute, but General Barksdale galloped along the line, and said: "Boys, Harper's Ferry has surrendered." A yell went up, and the enemy fell back in the valley. Our march to Harper's Ferry began, and as we started, the enemy opened on us with his artillery. Our wagons and servants were two or three miles ahead of us, and were ordered to move before we reached them. A Negro had been left on the side of the road asleep, and was there as we passed; but of course we had no knowledge of it. The shells were falling on all sides. One struck the ground very near the sleeping Negro. He had two or three canteens, a frying-pan, and a camp-kettle strapped around his neck. He rushed by, making as much noise as a train of cars. Nobody could attract his attention. He was flying. Finally a man grabbed him, and asked: "What is the matter?" "Lord, I seed the cannon bust, and I hearn the bum-er coming. Marster, lemme go."

We reached Harper's Ferry in a short time, and found that General Jackson was already paroling the prisoners. We remained on the Maryland side until next morning, Tuesday, September 16, 1862, when we crossed and occupied the street. Here we were given five hard-tacks each. We moved at 4 P. M., supposedly for the charming valley of the Shenandoah, to rest and enjoy our victories.

CHAPTER EIGHT

The Army Recrosses the Potomac – The Potomac –
The Battle of Sharpsburg – General Sims Wounded –
D. H. Hill and His Nerve

Tuesday, September 16, 1862, McLaws' division, composed of Kershaw's South Carolina, Cobb's Georgia, Sims' Georgia, and Barksdale's Mississippi brigades, stood in the streets of Harper's Ferry all day. About four o'clock in the afternoon, we received orders to move. The column headed south. We supposed that, having captured so many prisoners at Harper's Ferry, we were going into the beautiful valley of Virginia for rest and rations. The men moved along at a lively gait. As night came on, we sang all kinds of plantation songs, "Rock the Cradle, Julie," "Sallie, Get Your Hoe Cake Done," "I'm Gwying down the Newburg Road," and so on. The men were scattered for two miles along the road. The woods rang with their melodies. We had passed through a severe campaign, comprising many hard-fought battles, and marched several hundred miles with very scant rations. The scenes we had passed through in the last two months were dreadful. Not a man in the division but had lost a dear friend, or maybe a relative, and their bodies had been buried in a long trench without a shroud. Ordinarily, this would be a solemn and mournful retrospection, but these were not ordinary times, nor ordinary men. The times were eventful and the men were heroes, who realized that there was no sentiment in war, and that they must meet the trials and bear the sufferings incident to hostilities between two great armies. When we go back to those scenes, we are amazed at the fortitude and endurance of those men. On they marched, singing at the top of their voices, dreaming of the good "ash cakes" and "apple butter" we had heard so much about down at Winchester, Strasburg, and other places in the valley, when suddenly we came to where the road forked. The column turned into the right-hand road. As each company filed into the changed direction, their melodious voices were hushed. They knew that the war was not over. They realized that we would recross the Potomac, and that this meant fight. Within half an hour, not a sound could be heard except the din of the moving artillery. All the humor and bright anticipations of an hour ago were gone. The men were silent, but determined. Very soon the head of the column quickened the pace, and we were forced to trot nearly all the remainder of the night to keep up. The step was growing rapid. Hundreds of good men could not keep it.

About daylight we reached Shepardstown on the Potomac river, and crossed over to the Maryland side, but we crossed with a small proportion of the command which began the march. We remember that Company "C," Eighteenth Mississippi, left Harper's Ferry with over sixty men and three officers, but we went into the battle of "Sharpsburg" with sixteen men and one officer. Other companies, of course, suffered similar dimunition. The march was one of the severest ever made by infantry troops. About thirty miles in fourteen hours. The river at Shepardstown is over a half mile wide, and very shoaly. A gallant little Irishman, belonging to Company "C," Eighteenth Mississippi Regiment, Tommy Brennan, never played out. He was one of the sixteen who crossed the river. He was of very small stature, but brave as a lion. In crossing he held his gun, cartridge box and shoes on his head to prevent them from getting wet. When within about twenty yards of the shore, he hallooed out: "Boys, I am over dry shod." But as he looked back to make the announcement he stepped into a deep hole, and went under head and ears, gun and all. When he arose he said, as if to finish the remark: "After I get on some dry clothes."

We soon arrived at Sharpsburg. The battle was raging. We

halted in the roadway of the little town. We were given thirty minutes to rest. Two men were detailed from each company to fill the canteens. The little Confederate and W. L. McKee were detailed from Company "C," and by the time we returned the order to march was given. We double-quicked about a mile, and reached a grove of large trees. Our line was formed, General Barksdale rode in front and addressed the men thus: "The situation is desperate. The enemy is pressing the center. We must drive them back, Stonewall Jackson says so. I want every man to do his duty as a Mississippian. If any of you can not, step out, and I will excuse you." Not a man moved. It was a trying ordeal. The shells were flying thick, and we knew in a moment numbers of us would be killed, but the endurance that stood the men so well on the march from Harper's Ferry would hold them now. General Barksdale then said: "Pile every thing except guns and cartridge boxes at this tree. There were about seven or eight blankets in the brigade. They constituted the pile. While we stood here, General D. H. Hill galloped up on a yellow horse, about one hundred yards in our front, and halted. He dropped the reins and took out his field glasses and watched the enemy. Major Ratchford, his adjutant general, joined him. In a moment a shell passed through the general's horse. The horse was killed instantly; he never kicked. General Hill did not move the glass from his eyes, but shaking the stirrups from his feet stepped a few paces off and continued watching the enemy without the slightest emotion. Major Ratchford dismounted and removed the saddle and bridle from the dead horse. Finally, General Hill mounted Major Ratchford's horse and rode off. This was characteristic of D. H. Hill. Nothing could excite him. He was the coolest man in our army. We have seen General S. D. Lee in hot places, and have since the war spoken to him of his nerve, but he answered: "D. H. Hill was the coolest man I ever knew. I took lessons from him."

"Left-face," "forward march," rang out, and we moved by columns toward the center of our lines. "Left front, into line" was repeated by the company officers all along. We moved at double-quick across plowed ground, and formed line behind a high rail fence, just at the edge of a beautiful wood. As our line advanced to position we passed General Robert E. Lee. He sat on his horse near a battery of the Richmond Howitzers, which was actively engaged. We cheered him as we passed. The shell and shot were pounding the earth and cutting down the timber. Men were falling at every step. It was dreadful. A spotted cow ran through the line, going to our rear. She ran like a race horse; her tail was high in the air. A shell struck the ground a few feet in her front and exploded. The dirt went in all directions and left a big hole, into which she plunged, but scrambled out, continuing her race in the same direction. Kit Gilmer, of Company "C," hallooed out: "Boys, she's a Confederate cow, she's going South." We remained behind a fence about five minutes. Ransom's North Carolina brigade was in our front. The shells were shrieking, the grape shots were whizzing, and the minnies were sizzing. The fence was nearly shot down. The North Carolinians were being driven back. They fought desperately, but were overpowered. We waited in awful suspense. In a moment we would rise to meet the vanquishers of Ransom's men. "Press forward, Mississippians," came from proud General Kershaw. Ransom's men pressed through our ranks. We rushed at the enemy with a yell, and drove them back, almost reaching the top of the hill. We were now in large timber. The enemy fell back to their temporary works of logs and brush. Our line halted. General Barksdale rushed to the front and said, "Forward! take the works!" Two minutes afterward, we stood on the top of them and shot the enemy as he ran down the hill. We had checked the enemy's attack on our army's center, and had driven him back. Our line advanced about two miles. The day was won.

    McLaws' division met General Lee's expectations, but some of the noblest men who ever lived gave their lives to the cause in that battle. Sharpsburg was one of the bloodiest as well as one of the most stubbornly contested battles of the war. An idea of the loss can be gained by a comparison of Company "C" Eighteenth Mississippi regiment. Of the sixteen men and a lieutenant who took part in the battle, six were killed and five were wounded, leaving five men and a lieutenant. Sam W. Finley, Pleasant Smith, James E. Burns, W. L. McKee, and the Little Con-

Suddenly a Shell Exploded in Their Midst

Confederate, together with Lieutenant Wm. McKie, were the survivors. The battle was fought on Wednesday, September 17, 1862. The weather was pleasant. We used the muzzle-loading gun, and had to bite off the end of the cartridge. Our hands and faces were as black as the powder. About 4 P.M. we were lying in an apple orchard. The enemy, in our front, were lying behind a stone fence about six hundred yards distant. The artillery on both sides was keeping up a desultory firing. The enemy's shell would occasionally knock off a limb from an apple tree. We ate apples as long as we could swallow them. Billy McKee and the Little Confederate worked their way to a branch, which ran between the lines, and filled their canteens. Generals J.E.B. Stuart, Cobb, Kershaw, Sims, and Barksdale stood about fifty yards in front of our regiment watching the enemy behind the rock fence. The Little Confederate was watching the group. Suddenly a shell exploded in their midst. General Sims fell backward heavily to the ground. The Little Confederate rushed to him, placing his canteen of water to the general's mouth. General Sims clutched the canteen and chattered it against his teeth. In a moment Sam Finley caught him by one arm, and the Little Confederate took the other, and then pulled him down the hill, and out of range of the shells. The other generals followed, but found that it was only a bad powder burn, and resumed their positions. Soon a litter arrived, and General Sims was carried to the rear.

    We lay in our position all night, during which time numbers of those who broke down on the march from Harper's Ferry caught up and fell into line. About two o'clock in the morning, the Little Confederate was awakened by Matt, who had a canteen of buttermilk and a good sized ash cake. Lieutenant McKie, Sam Finley, Billy McKee, Jim Burns, and Pleas. Smith, together with the Little Confederate, certainly enjoyed that banquet. We could never learn how Matt found us in that long line of battle. Thursday we remained on the field within sight of the enemy's lines. Friday, September 19th, we moved off towards Shepardstown. As we marched along, the Little Confederate noticed General Sims near the way sitting on his horse. He spoke of the circumstance of the shell to some of his friends who caught up after the battle.

General Sims noticed him, and asked, "Are you the boy who gave me the water and helped to carry me off the field Wednesday?" The little fellow stopped to answer the general's question. The latter said, "Would you like to go with me as courier?"

"No, sir," said the boy, "I would rather stay with my company."

The general then asked his name, also his company and regiment, and where he lived, but he could not persuade him to leave his company. We passed a large stone barn, where the wounded of Barksdale's brigade had been taken. Among the wounded was "Kit Gilmer." A bullet passed through his leg crushing the bones. Kit was a remarkable boy, and his father was a remarkable man; fear never found a lodgment in their hearts. It was understood that our army was to recross the Potomac, and that the wounded would be left behind. Kit had a Negro named "Ike." After dark, Ike pressed the good old farmer's horse, put his young master on him, got behind, and never dismounted until they reached Winchester. The suffering was intense, but Kit never murmured. The strange sequel of this story is that Ike went back with the horse, and remained with the Federal army. We captured him back at Fredericksburg, and he is living in Madison county, Mississippi, now.

CHAPTER NINE
☆ ☆ ☆ ☆

The Army Goes Into Camp at Winchester –
Small-Pox Breaks Out – The March to Fredericksburg –
The Enemy Capture Barksdale's Works, But Are
Driven Back – The Washington Artillery Cheer
Barksdale's Mississippi Brigade – Billy Blake and a
Little Dog Frighten the People in Church

The army crossed the river and went into camp at Winchester. Soon afterward a bad spell of weather came on, and the last of September quite a snow fell. We had no blankets, and very few clothes. To add to the hardships and horrors of the situation, small-pox broke out, and fully one-third of the army had it. The Little Confederate and Matt were taken at the same time, while Uncle Freeman escaped. The soldiers never thought much about the danger of small-pox, but the Negroes who had it suffered greatly. Matt never recovered from the effects, though he lived twenty years afterward. He was always complaining and suffered to the last with rheumatism. We spent a week or so delightfully at Winchester, but our dream of happiness was short, and we moved to Strasburg, thence via Rapidan Station to Fredericksburg. It began to rain and sleet just before we reached Rapidan, where we forded the river and marched nearly all night in the cold and sleet. By next morning the weather had become bitter cold, and whenever we halted ten minutes our clothing would freeze on our bodies. We were hurried every step of the way to Fredericksburg. The command of the Army of the Potomac during the three months had been transferred to General Pope, then to Meade, then back to McClellan, and now we learned that General Burnside was in command. We were marching night and day to reach Fredericksburg to prevent his crossing the Rappahannock. McLaws' division was the first to reach there, about ten o'clock at night; it was still sleeting, and very cold. We were not allowed to have fires, lest the enemy might be enabled to estimate our forces, as we were told. We were freezing. We lay down on each other, four men at the bottom, four men across them, then four men on top these. It was generally in piles of twelve. After the bottom quartette thawed out, they would go on top, and so on. We spent two miserable days and nights before the army arrived; then we had fires. Rations were issued almost daily at that time, but one man could eat at one meal all the rations drawn by a mess of six or seven men for a day. We began to fortify, and at night the scene was grand. The camp-fires of both armies made a beautiful picture, the opposing forces being within plain view of each other. On one occasion when the Eighteenth Mississippi Regiment was on picket duty, the Little Confederate and Jeff Crane were on post together, and stood behind trees on the bank of the river. We shot at every thing that moved, as did the enemy. If a hat was raised, a bullet whizzed at it. While we watched, a Negro appeared just in front of the Little Confederate; he seemed to have sprung out of the ground. He carried a sack on his back, and both Crane and the Little Confederate ordered him to lie down. He said he belonged to the Colonel of the Eighth Georgia, and had been out foraging, and why the enemy's pickets did not kill him I am unable to conjecture. The Little Confederate made him open his bag, in which he had a bushel of sweet potatoes. He was only required to empty out half of them. Jeff Crane and his little friend went back to camp that night with most of the half bushel of raw potatoes in their "craws."

  Several weeks passed at Fredericksburg in getting ready to entertain General Burnside when he should cross the "beautiful Rappahannock." During that time the soldiers of both armies became very friendly. The Confederates would send tobacco in

Traffic on the Rappahannock

little bark boats over to the "Yanks," and the latter would send us back coffee and other articles. It finally got so that the pickets would not shoot at each other. The men became very expert in setting the sails on the bark, which they could land at almost the very place they selected for the exchange of commodities. It was a strange sight to watch the men of opposing armies playing and trafficking as if there was no war, but they were ready to face each at any minute, and fight like lions and tigers if the orders were given. Weeks were quietly spent on the beautiful river; Barksdale's Mississippi brigade was moved into the streets of Fredericksburg, where they remained until the great battle. Our artillery was planted on Marye's Heights overlooking the whole country. When General Burnside built his bridge under cover of darkness, and moved his army over to the south side, he began setting the pegs for a great and bloody battle, and he got it.

      The battle of Fredericksburg will go down in history, crowned with some remarkable features, but of these there was nothing more striking than the part Barksdale's brigade bore in the conflict. The position this brigade held could not be surrendered; it was necessary to maintain it at all hazards; the safety of our army depending, in a measure, on their doing so. It was the key to the situation, the bulwark of the army, and it was a high compliment to the Mississippi brigade to have such an important duty assigned to it. General Burnside knew that he must break our line at this point, otherwise he would be forced to recross the river. He, therefore, concentrated the fire of four hundred cannon on Barksdale's brigade, before his infantry made the memorable charge. I believe I can say, with absolute confidence, there was not a square yard of earth in the city of Fredericksburg which was not struck during that awful cannonading. Hundreds of old soldiers who saw the determination of the Federal commander to annihilate Barksdale's brigade looked on in wonder. How could the men stand it? It has been discussed ever since, and will be a theme as long as there is a man living who participated in or witnessed it. The charge of Pickett's brigade at Gettysburg was terrible, but it was nothing to the storm which rained on Barksdale's dale's brigade at Fredericksburg. Pickett's men were on the move, they were the attacking party, and there was the inspiration of General Lee's presence. The Mississippians stood at Fredericksburg exposed to the greatest artillery fire they had ever known, and with hardly a hope that it would cease till the last of the gallant band had fallen. Writers tell of Pickett's charge, and it "will live in song and story" forever, and it is due to those brave and gallant soldiers that it shall so live. A towering monument of finest marble should be reared to commemorate their heroic sacrifices and their sublime devotion even unto death. Every name should be inscribed upon it. The descendants of those heroes can refer with pride in all ages to the heroism their ancestors displayed in that grand and terrific charge. It will be an object lesson for future generations, inspiring the youth of every nationality to build his life on such a foundation, as will enable him to approach the grand heroism of those great "Virginians." But it required more courage, more manhood, and more heroism to face the situation which Barksdale and his Mississippians faced at Fredericksburg than to follow the charge at Gettysburg.

After that artillery hell, Barksdale's brigade was moved down into the valley, and deployed a skirmish line along the river bank. The men marched through the crooked streets in column of fours. From a distance it looked like a long snake; there was perfect order and steadiness, and the entire army was struck with it. Notwithstanding the awful situation in which they had been for two days, they moved with proud military bearing. As they emerged into the valley, a great cheer went up from Marye's Heights, where General Lee had stationed the Washington artillery. We have heard men say they never saw such remarkable nerve in all their lives. Any soldier who witnessed that cannonading, it matters not whether he be Federal or Confederate, will tell you it was the most terrific during the war, and we believe of any war. The Federals crossed during the night. Barksdale's brigade was at the foot of the hill to meet them. They rushed at our line like droves of wolves. Hundreds were killed, but the line preserved its order. It was an awful occasion. The position held by Barksdale must be taken. The enemy charged us, and fought like devils. Theirs was a grand command as well as ours. They were

"Americans." They attempted to climb over our little temporary ditch, which was a breast-work in name only, but we clubbed them with our guns, and drove them back. They were reinforced and re-formed. The Washington artillery poured shell right into their ranks. They opened but closed up again. We saw them move forward the second time under the fire of the batteries, as well as our infantry fire. They reached our lines again. It seemed as if the fate of the human race depended on the conduct of each individual. Every man in both armies stood square to the front. Many gallant deeds were performed by individuals, almost every man on both sides deserved special mention, but there was a circumstance that did not at the time seem unusual, which should be mentioned. Company "C" of the Eighteenth regiment was the color company. The flag was planted squarely on the bank of the ditch, and the enemy directed a deadly fire on it. The color bearer was killed, another man grabbed the staff and raised it. He, too, was killed, and several others followed and were also killed. The enemy was within ten feet of the flag, making it almost certain death for any man to raise it. A modest fellow whose place was near the center of our company – Luke W. Smith – rushed at the colors and raised them just as the enemy climbed the bank. The flag had been shot in probably a hundred places. A Federal soldier attempted to take it from him; but Luke Smith, though slender, made up his mind to hold on to that staff as long as he lived, and his adversary was equally determined. The men on both sides had all they could attend to, and Luke and the Yankee scrambled and fought over the colors. Finally, the Yankee tore the fragments of the flag off the staff, leaving Luke with nothing but the stick. We again drove the enemy back, and as they retired Luke broke the staff over his antagonist's head, and recovered the flag, but he never gave up the piece he held in his hands.

General Burnside re-crossed the river and resumed his position. The Little Confederate remembered the stories his father had told him about hardships he endured when a boy. He told of how he had to sleep in the covered wagons when he was going to Charleston, South Carolina, with his mother's cotton. The snow would blow in on his blankets, and sometimes cover them while he slept. They seemed great hardships, and his father would say: "I hope you will never be called on to endure the like." But at seventeen years of age, the little fellow could tell his father stories of hardships, dangers, sufferings and trials, he had never dreamed of. He wrote home after each battle, and recited the distressful news of the death of his friends. He was getting terribly tired of the business, but never a murmur escaped him. The first battle of Fredricksburg was fought December 12 and 13, 1862.

Notwithstanding this terrible and bloody battle, scarcely two weeks passed before the army had settled down to a normal condition. One would not suppose that in so short a time after they had fought with such desperation, and seen so many of their friends killed and wounded by their sides, men could be cheerful and hopeful. But this was a remarkable characteristic of the Confederate soldier. He could throw off trouble, or face dangers, as occasion demanded. Merry laughter and jests could be heard at every mess fire. The men sang and danced at night, and talked of home and lounged about during the day. It was impossible to break or even check their spirits. They attended divine service on Sunday and prayer meeting every other night – that is, they were supposed to do so. The chaplain of the regiment, Rev. A. E. Hackett, was in every sense a good man. He always went into battle with the regiment, and used a gun with telling effect. When the fight was over, he was found among the wounded, giving them every assistance within human power. He was dearly beloved by every man in the Eighteenth regiment. Many of us would go to hear his beautiful and touching prayers, because of his great earnestness.

Occasionally the men would go to church in the city. One night, soon after the battle, Billy Blake, John Willis, Lieutenant Wm. McKie, Winter Shipp and the Little Confederate went into town to attend church. Arriving there, they found the pews all filled, more than half of the congregation being soldiers. Lieutenant McKie and Winter Shipp went in and found seats, but Billy Blake, John Willis and the Little Confederate remained outside, near the entrance. They amused themselves in many ways, as best they could, while they waited for their friends to join them after the service was over. Finally a little dog came up and looked in the church door. He seemed to be hunting for his master. Willis tried to drive him away, but he was spunky and would not go. Billy Blake, who was always bubbling over with mischief, caught the dog and addressing the Little Confederate, said: "Little Horse, hold him until I can come back." He was off and back in a few minutes, with an old, battered tin bucket. He mashed the top together after putting a few pebbles in it, and with a string torn from his shirt, tied it to the dog's tail. The dog did not realize what was going on, but evidently thought he was being caressed. After it was all ready, Billy picked the dog up, carried him off some twenty yards, and put him down, supposing he would run down the street. They looked for great fun, but when he hit the ground he knew something was wrong, and instead of going home, he broke for the church. Down the aisle he ran with all his speed, the bucket striking the floor, making as much noise as a wagon train. He barked at every jump. It threw the congregation into great confusion. Men stood on their seats, and ladies screamed. The dog reached the pulpit. He had not found his master; not even a friendly hand. He rushed into the pulpit. It was all done in a second. The church was poorly lighted with tallow candles, one resting on each side of the Bible. As the dog reached the pulpit, the preacher jumped up on the desk, knocking off the candles and extinguishing them. The dog started down the other aisle, and by this time the greatest excitement prevailed. Men jumped out of the windows, others rushed through the doors. The occasion was so unusual and so unexpected, the best soldiers were knocked completely out. The three boys saw the dog go up in the pulpit, saw the lights go out, and witnessed the confusion, then broke for camp. They ran as rapidly as they could for nearly a mile before they halted or said a word. When they pulled up, Billy Blake, in the most solemn manner said: "Little Horse, what did you start that derned dog toward the church for?" and then fell down and rolled over in the road. They laughed and talked about it until they heard others approaching, when they put out again. They reached camp, and lay down in front of the fire on the bare ground, and pretended to be asleep. Directly the church goers began to arrive, and the balance of our crowd with them. Lieutenant McKie knew, as soon as he saw them all hugged up together before the fire, who tied the can to the dog, but he never accused the boys. The occurrence was the talk of the camp, as well as of the good citizens of Fredericksburg. Next day General Barksdale instructed each colonel to investigate the matter fully, and if it was found to have been done by a man of his brigade, he wanted the scamp well punished. The boys were the only persons who seemed entirely ignorant of the trouble.

Uncle Freeman was in the church, and in the mad rush he lost his haversack. He always carried it over his shoulder. The one he lost he prized greatly. It was a nice one, he found on a dead Yankee officer at Sharpsburg. Uncle Freeman had said very little about the affair, and was very cold toward "Billy" and "Bud." Finally, Billy asked him if he knew who tied the bucket to the dog's tail. He said: "I know 'zactly who done it, jis' as good if I'd er seed um, and, Mars Billy, you knows who dun it too." Billy assumed a most pathetic air, referred to his good intentions in going to church, how it grieved him to be accused of so horrible an act, and hoped that God would forgive Uncle Freeman for his cruel and wicked suspicion against the boys. Billy was so earnest that he finally convinced Uncle Freeman of their innocence. The boys were very quiet and good for a few days, but were soon out roving over the country for something to eat during the day, and making life a burden to their friends at night.

CHAPTER TEN

The Men of Both Armies Become Very Friendly – The Little Confederate is Appointed First Lieutenant in the C. S. Army, and Presents Himself to the Secretary of War

There was no characteristic in the American soldier more prominent than his ability to adapt himself to circumstances. It was but a short time after the battle of Fredericksburg, where the two armies had been arrayed against each other with all the ferocity of wolves, and yet the men on both sides were perfectly friendly as individuals. "The Yanks" sent us newspapers, coffee and other things they could get, and we sent them tobacco. We had nothing else they wanted. The neighborly feeling was growing, till the officers thought it was going too far, and ordered us to stop all communications, and to shoot at every man we saw. But all the bitterness was forgotten, and it was impossible to stop us from being friendly toward each other.

Oftentimes you would hear a Confederate halloo, "Hello, Old Yank! how you getting on?"

The Yank would answer: "All right Old Johnnie, what's the news?"

"Say, Old Yank, send me a newspaper and some coffee."

"All right, Old Johnnie. Wait a minute. Say, I'm going off duty now, I will see you again to-morrow good bye," and other such chats.

I have seen dozens of old Johnnies, and as many Yanks, kneeling at the river's edge, getting their bark boats in position to send over. The kindest feeling prevailed, and I venture to assert, though it has been a long time since then, that the war could have been settled in ten days if the question had been left to the soldiers. The Federal soldier had a profound regard for the Southern soldier after the battle of Fredericksburg. It was right here that the loftiest sentiment ever suggested to a soldier's mind came out. It was in the spring of 1863.

> Two great armies were encamped on either side of the Rappahannock river, one dressed in blue and the other in grey. As twilight fell, the bands on the Union side began to play "The Star Spangled Banner," and "Rally Round the Flag." The challenge was taken up by those on the other side and they responded with "The Bonnie Blue Flag," and "Away Down South in Dixie." It was borne upon the soul of a single soldier in one of those bands to begin a sweeter, more tender air, and, slowly as he played it, all the instruments on the Union side joined in, until finally a great and mighty chorus swelled up all along the lines of both armies, "Home Sweet Home." When they had finished there was no challenge yonder, for every band upon that farther shore had taken up the sweet old air, so attuned to all that is holiest and dearest in human nature, and one chorus of the two hosts went up to God. When the music had ceased, from the boys in grey came a challenge: "Three cheers for Home." And as they went resounding toward the skies from both sides of the river, something upon the soldiers' cheeks washed off the stains of powder.

Could such a circumstance occur in any country in the world except our own? None but Americans can understand the feelings of the soldiers of those great armies. The men who had faced each other but a few weeks ago in one of the bloodiest battles of the world, could now be marshaled under one banner on a mere suggestion.

On one occasion, the Little Confederate was busy getting his bark ready to sail. He was squatting at the river's edge, instead of standing picket, as he was told to do, when the corporal of the guard, Lem. Harvey, spoke to him and said: "The captain wants you. I will take your post."

The little fellow reported to his captain, who, in turn, ordered him to report to General Barksdale. "What have I done?" he asked himself.

Arriving at the general's fire, he saluted, and said: "General, I was ordered to report to you."

He probably noticed the boy was nervous, and said: "Little Horse, what have you been doing? I thought you would get into trouble. Come along with me."

The general and the boy walked off together. He was a friend of the boy's father, but the little fellow thought his time had come. They reached the camp of General Sims' Georgia brigade, and halted at the general's fire. General Barksdale said: "Here is the 'Little Horse.'" And turning to the boy, asked: "Do you know General Sims?"

The little fellow thought General Sims was a witness against him, so he answered: "No, sir."

"Why," said the general, "are you not the boy who gave me the water when I was hurt at Sharpsburg, and helped me off the field?"

He could not deny this.

"Well," said General Sims, "I have often thought of you, and it affords me much pleasure to say you have been appointed a lieutenant in the Confederate States Army, and here is your commission;" at the same time handing an official envelope addressed to The Hon. James A. Sedden, Secretary of War, Richmond, Va.

The boy was so astounded it was several minutes before he could speak. He took the letter, which looked fully as large as a front door. It was the first official envelope he had ever seen. Finally he thanked the general, who said: "General Barksdale will give you transportation to Richmond, and after you have presented yourself to the Secretary of War, he will give you permission to go home a few days."

It seemed like a dream. The little fellow was anxious to get away, for fear somebody would tell him it was a joke. He went back to his company, and all arrangements were made for his departure. He did not have a dollar, but Captain Frank Cassell gave him $150 to take to his brother, who lived at Canton, Miss.

It was Wednesday morning that Uncle Freeman, Matt, and the "Little Soldier" took the train for Richmond. They arrived about five in the afternoon, and went to the Spottswood Hotel, which was thought to be the best, as well as the most expensive, hotel in Richmond. The boy and his two Negroes marched in. They stood and looked. They had never seen such a grand place before. In a few moments, a man approached the trio, and, pointing to the door, said: "Get out of here." The Little Confederate had long yellow hair, badly tangled and matted. He had the rim of a hat, no top or brim to it, simply a band; the waist of an old coat (the skirt had been cut off to patch the sleeves, and for other uses); a pair of old Yankee pants, the left leg split from the knee down, and tied together with willow bark. You could see his mangy skin, and, what was worse than all, he was full of "gray backs." Ben Muse had given him the legs of a pair of boots, which he had tied together at both ends and cut a hole in the middle; these were his shoes he had no socks. No wonder the hotel man ordered him out.

They stood in the street a short time, but it was very cold, and Matt went to find a place for shelter. Very soon he returned, and they went down into the kitchen of the hotel, where they ate the scraps from the table and went to sleep on the stone floor. Next morning, the good old Negro cook gave them breakfast, and the little fellow and his Negroes, whom he loved more than himself, started for the capitol. They waited some time before the offices were open, after which they looked about to find Mr. Sedden. Presently Uncle Freeman, who could read, noticed a sign on a door. "Office of Secretary of War." The little soldier knocked. A guard sat inside, with a gun across his lap. He asked abruptly: "What do you want?"

"I want to see the Secretary of War. I have a letter for him."

"Give it to me; I will send it in," said the guard."

"No; I was told to give it to him myself." This seemed to make the guard mad, and he said: "Get away from here, you ragged scamp," and closed the door.

Uncle Freeman and Matt, were furious. Uncle Freeman

The Little Confederate and His Negroes
As They Appeared Before the Secretary of State

said: "He better not let marster hear him say that. Called my young marster a ragged scamp! I like to know how many niggers he got. I bet marster's got more niggers and mules and oxen than he got in his whole neighborhood. I know he is. Called my marster ragged! I don't care if he is ragged, he shan't call him ragged. I gwine to tell marster, if God spares me."

While Uncle Freeman talked, Matt, was getting hot. If the little fellow had said the word, Matt would have smashed the door down. They went back from the War Department badly discouraged. Passing along the street, they saw the "Mississippi Supply Depot." Dr. W. W. Devine, a friend of the boy, was in charge, and, after listening to the boy's story, said: "You come here about ten o'clock tomorrow, and I will go with you." The day was spent in the kitchen of the Spottswood.

Promptly at ten o'clock Friday, the little soldier and his two Negroes were waiting the doctor's pleasure. Soon he was ready, and they proceeded to the capitol. The little fellow knocked at the door where the same guard was on duty.

"Are you here again?" he asked.

"Yes," answered Dr. Devine, "and he is going in, too."

The guard moved his chair. Dr. Devine passed into an adjoining room where he introduced the Little Confederate; Uncle Freeman and Matt standing close behind. Mr. Sedden was dressed in dark clothes; his spectacles were tied back of his head, the rim resting on his nose. He resembled D. H. Hill, and did not seem to need the glasses, for he looked over them. He opened the large envelope, and questioned the boy about where he lived, his father's name and address.

The secretary and Dr. Devine passed into another room, and when they returned, he said, "Have you no better clothing than those you have on?"

"No, sir," answered the boy.

"Well," said Mr. Sedden, "you go with these gentlemen" (referring to Dr. Devine and a man from his office) "and they will try to get you a better suit. After you do so, come back to see me; by that time I will have your papers ready."

As they left the room, Mr. Sedden said, "Have his hair cut

also." There is no doubt that he was about as "onery" looking a chap as ever entered the Confederate capitol. He might have had "cockle-burs" in his hair, but he didn't, and that was the only thing wanting to complete the awkwardness of his appearance. Nor was he an exception. The army for the past five months had been very actively engaged, and nothing in the way of clothing could reach the men.

Our party passed several streets, finally went into a clothing store, where tailors were busy making uniforms. The gentleman from Mr. Sedden's office selected a suit of underwear, shoes and socks, and a suit of clothes. He had them wrapped up in a bundle and left the store. Soon they passed down into a cellar; it was a barber-shop and bath-room. The gentleman said to the Negro attendant, "Get a bar of good soap, and give this young man a thorough cleaning," then turning to the barber, said, "You cut his hair." He left the bundle of clothes and said to the boy, "Throw your old ones away and put the new ones on."

After the boy had stripped, the Negro walked in with a bar of home-made lye soap; one side of it had the coarse salt sticking out. He evidently thought it was a case which needed heroic treatment. The boy had stood insults from the clerk in the hotel, and from the guard at the door of the Secretary of War's office, but when he told that nigger not to rub him so hard with that old rough soap, he meant it. It required Uncle Freeman and Matt, also the barber, to pull the boy loose from that nigger. He yelled like a goat. Uncle Freeman had to finish the job. After leaving the barber-shop, the three promenaded the streets till night came on, when they went back to the Spotswood. Uncle Freeman and Matt were very proud of their young "marster" now, and admired him extravagantly. Uncle Freeman said, "Wonder what that guard up yonder to the White House gwine to say now."

Reaching the hotel, a man said, " Come in. Will you register?"

"Will I do what! What did you say to me?" asked the little soldier.

"Walk up to the counter and register," he answered. The

little fellow never heard the expression before. While he had stopped at hotels, it was always with his father and mother, and he had no idea what register meant. He consulted Uncle Freeman and Matt.

Uncle Freeman said, "Don't you do it! Don't you do it."

So the boy walked up to the man and said, "I won't do it, sir; I never did such a thing in my life. I don't drink nor play cards either."

The man laughed and said, "That is not what I meant. Come up here and write your name, so I can give you a room."

The following day was Saturday. When the little soldier rapped at the office door of the Secretary of War, the same guard opened it, but he opened it wide, and was very courteous. Reaching Mr. Sedden's presence, he saluted and said, "Mr. Sedden, I have returned for the papers."

"What papers; I do not think I know you."

The boy explained, but Mr. Sedden replied, "Do not try to deceive me; the young man who brought these papers looked very differently from you." The secretary teased the boy for some minutes, then addressing him as "lieutenant," gave him his commission, dated April the 9th, 1863, together with transportation for himself and Negroes to Canton, Mississippi. He also gave him orders to report to Lieutenant-General Pemberton at Vicksburg, and a leave of absence for thirty days to visit his "dear mother and father."

The whole affair seemed so much like Jack and his beanstalk that the little fellow scarcely knew whether it was a reality or not. He did not thank Mr. Sedden for the clothes, it did not occur to him until after the train left Richmond, but some weeks after he reached home, his father received a letter from General Barksdale inclosing the bills. The general had requested Mr. Sedden to fit the young "lieutenant" out. In future we will refer to the Little Confederate as "Lieutenant Bleecker."

CHAPTER ELEVEN

The Little Confederate Leaves the Army of
Northern Virginia, and Spends a Few Weeks at Home

    Lieutenant Bleecker, before leaving Richmond, spent a day at the hospitals, where several of his friends had been taken after the battle of Fredericksburg. A gallant young fellow from Madison county, David Saddler, was a member of the Twenty-first Mississippi Regiment, Barksdale's brigade. At Fredericksburg he had one of his feet shot off by a cannon ball. A friend offered to take him back where the surgeons could give him attention, but Dave said: "No, not now; but after you have driven them back across the river, come and help me." The friend was James L. Finley, a friend also of Lieutenant Bleecker. In less than ten minutes, Jim Finley had his right arm shot off above the elbow, and as he was leaving the field passed the spot where he had left Dave Saddler, and found to his great horror that his other foot had been shot off, and that he was bleeding to death. Be it ever said to the praise of Jim Finley, that he forgot his own sufferings, and hurried back to report the fact to the colonel, exposing himself to a terrific fire in doing so. A detail was sent, which carried both Saddler and Finley to the field hospital. These two boys were in the hospital at Richmond when Lieutenant Bleecker called. They were all warm friends, and enjoyed being together. Mrs. Owens, a devoted sister of Dave Saddler, went from Madison county to nurse him, and it was largely due to her tender care that those boys survived. They are both living to-day, David Saddler at Corinth, Miss., and Jim Finley is the Rev. Dr. James L. Finley, a Baptist minister of much prominence.

These boys lay on their cots convalescing. A minister approached Dave Saddler, and offering him a nice pair of yarn socks, said: "Accept these, I wish the dear woman who knit them could present them to you in person."

Dave replied: "Thank you, very kindly, but I have decided I will never wear another pair of socks while I live."

The preacher protested, and insisted, but Dave could not be persuaded to take them. Finally the preacher met Mrs. Owens, and told her how foolish her brother had acted.

"Why," exclaimed Mrs. Owens, "both of his feet have been shot off!"

The official records of the United States, that were made up from the reports of both armies, which are regarded as nearly correct as any thing of the kind can be, show there were enlisted during the entire war on the Confederate side a little less than six hundred thousand men. This includes teamsters, nurses, provost-guards, and every man engaged. The greatest number engaged in service at any time was three hundred and seventeen thousand men. The same records show that there were enlisted in the Federal army during the same time two million eight hundred and seventy-two thousand men, or over two million men more than the Confederates had. General Lee's force was reduced by death and other causes to eight thousand men for duty. He surrendered that number besides five thousand disabled men to General Grant at Appomattox. General Grant's army, to which General Lee surrendered, numbered one hundred and eighty-five thousand men. Those eight thousand men were all heroes like Dave Saddler and Jim Finley. There were numbers of men with whom Lieutenant Bleecker parted on leaving the Army of Northern Virginia, that, he never saw afterward. Their bones are bleaching in the valleys, on the mountains and hills of Virginia. Those men were martyrs to a principle and human rights, and they left to posterity honored names and unblemished reputations. They established for the world a standard of manhood never before equaled, and one which will not be excelled. The State of Mississippi would honor herself by establishing and preserving an imperishable memorial for her sons who were among those martyrs. Each individual deserves it. They gave their lives for the State, and the State should remember their sufferings, their devotion, and their heroic sacrifices. The present generation will never appreciate their heroism, but they will be remembered in the far-distant future.

In bidding good-bye to the great Army of Northern Virginia, referring particularly to Barksdale's brigade, we drop a tear to the memory of heroic General William Barksdale, brave, patriotic and kind. He was a statesman, and a hero. We saw him in battle, on the march, and in camp. He felt a personal interest in every man in his brigade; he was proud of his men, and never doubted them. He believed they would follow him, nor was he mistaken. He fell with his face to the foe. To the brave and soldierly Colonel Thomas Griffin, of the Eighteenth Mississippi; a model soldier, and the grandest colonel in the army. And Colonel John C. Fizer, of the Seventeenth; Major James Campbell of the Eighteenth; and all the field officers of that incomparable brigade. We knew Colonel Fizer when he was the adjutant of his regiment, and we knew him when he was the colonel. He filled to a high degree the most exalted idea of a dashing cavalier, and proud as a knight of the crusades. We have seen him at the head of his regiment, on that light bay, before reaching any position he was ordered to take, dash ahead and reconnoiter, then gallop back. His face would be radiant. He was always looking out for his men. He was the same courtly, elegant gentleman under fire that he was in camp, or on the march. Too much could not be said of Major Campbell, as cool and courageous as Hill, and as watchful as Stuart; comparatively a boy, he filled his position with great credit. He commanded the Eighteenth regiment at the battle of Sharpsburg, and was seriously wounded within a few feet of the enemy's lines. He afterward died on the field of battle. A more patriotic soul never took its flight to the unknown world.

This story would fill a volume, if all the virtues of the gallant men of Barksdale's brigade were chronicled in it. The writer wishes he had the capacity to do them full justice, but the future must and will recognize their unquestionable right to rank as brave, true and great men. There were, of course, some men who filled the measure to overflowing. Such were Captain W. G Johnson, Lieutenant Wm. McKie, Lieutenant George Covert, Sam Finley, James Burnes, Ed. Drenning, Peter Whalen, Bateman Brown, Peyton Wales, W. L. McKee, John Sneed, and others, all of Company "C," Eighteenth Mississippi regiment. These men never shirked duty, never straggled, never missed a march or a battle. They were an inspiration to the other men. We have been exhausted and felt that we could not go another hundred yards, but when we saw the earnest faces of those men, we found new life and energy. Sam Finley, Peyton Wales and Jim Burns were ideal soldiers; always ready for duty, without a complaint at any time. They were Christian soldiers of the grandest type. They passed through the entire war, until within a few weeks of its close, and were killed at Berryville, Virginia, at the same time, and side by side, as they had stood and fought for four long years. Providence seemed unwilling to separate them. W. L. McKee was a few months younger than Lieutenant Bleecker, and the only boy in the brigade who was. "Billy," as he was familiarly called by all the division, was as gallant a little "Reb" as ever mustered for duty. General Barksdale selected him from all the brigade as his courier. His conduct was an honor to his people. "Billy" is still living, but has moved to Texas. Captain W. G. Johnson now lives at Orlando, Florida; Lieutenant George Covert at Meridian, Mississippi; Peter Whalen in Madison county, Mississippi; and Ed. Drenning in Yazoo City, Mississippi; but the others I have named were killed in battle.

PART II

General James R. Chalmers

CHAPTER TWELVE

Lieutenant Bleecker Reports to General James R. Chalmers For Duty, and is Assigned to the Command of an Artillery Section

Lieutenant Bleecker and his faithful Negroes reached Canton, Miss., their home, about the latter part of April, 1863, having been detained at several places en route on account of washouts and other causes. The facilities for transportation were as poor at that time as they could well be. There was great rejoicing at Bleecker's home. The dear mother, who prayed every day for the safety of her boy, felt that her prayer had been granted. Every thing was done for his comfort and happiness. Entertainments were arranged for his pleasure, to which all the friends of the neighborhood were invited, and all were glad to see the little fellow safely at home. Old people, the friends and neighbors of his parents, would listen to the stories he told with great interest. They felt that the boy had passed through a wonderful period, and they longed to hear all he had to say. They would inquire anxiously after their sons and brothers whom he left in Virginia. His dear mother clung to him as if she could never let him go again; but she enjoyed the happiness of the present, and felt proud that her boy had won the compliments and promotion he had received. The sisters and little brothers enjoyed the presence of their soldier brother, but after awhile began to think mother was partial to "Bud." We can see her heavenly face now, when she would place her arms around his neck and caress him with sweet tenderness. One of the most delightful months of his life was spent at this time.

Toward the middle of May, he saw his time was about up, and he must report to General Pemberton. Arriving at Vicksburg, he found every thing ready for an attack from the Federal fleet and army. He remained about the general's headquarters for several days waiting assignment, and finally, obtaining an interview, he asked to be assigned to General J.R. Chalmers, who had command of the cavalry in North Mississippi. The request was graciously granted, and he left Vicksburg just in time to escape the siege. He again returned home, for his horses and Negroes, where he spent a few days before reporting to General Chalmers. When he decided on the day he would go, his father said he must take two other Negroes, Jim and Burton, in place of Uncle Freeman and Matt. He felt that the latter had suffered hardships enough. He could not furnish a substitute for his son, but he could relieve the good old Negroes with substitutes.

Jim and Burton were delighted, and made promises that they would take care of "young marster" and bring him back home. When the day arrived, Lieutenant Bleecker, dressed in a new uniform, with a beautiful sword and belt, mounted on the handsomest little thoroughbred sorrel we ever saw, stood in the front yard to bid the dear ones goodbye again. Jim and Burton were also mounted on good horses, and were in the greatest state of excitement, talking to the Negroes, about a hundred or more, who had gathered around to say "good-bye." Jim's mother was Lieutenant Bleecker's "black mammy." She loved her white child devotedly, even more than she did her own. She clung to his feet, crying and praying for his safety and early return. It was a remarkable scene, and the most trying one that Bleecker was ever called on to go through. His dear mother delayed the departure from moment to moment, unable to give up her boy. The children and friends who were there to say "good-bye," crying and yelling, his old "black mammy" crying and holding on to him; while the old family Negroes were standing around, anxious to see the last of him. He had faced the enemy's guns, had seen friends killed or wounded by his side, but he never was tried so severely as now.

Finally the start was made. He realized that he must move quickly, or his strength of will might fail. Giving the little sorrel a pressure of the knee, he bounded off like a deer, followed by Jim and Burton, also well mounted. The Negroes ran down to the "big gate," hallooing "Good-bye, good-bye." The lieutenant rode in advance of his Negroes, unwilling to engage in conversation, which he knew Jim and Burton would want to do. Soon they arrived at the depot and boarded the train for Grenada. Jim and Burton rode in the car with the horses and were happy, while their young master lived over and over, and over again, the scenes of the past month. He looked out of the car window; he could not trust himself to talk, nor did he want the current of his thoughts disturbed. After a night spent at Grenada, he took the train for Panola, Miss., a small town on the Tallahatchie river. Arriving there together with his Negroes, he reported to General Chalmers, who read the order, and received him with the greatest kindness; so much so, that the lieutenant felt at home at once. He realized that he was in the presence of an accomplished gentleman, who would appreciate any efforts he made to do his duty.

After the introduction to the members of his staff, the general said: "Lieutenant, we are expecting the enemy to make an attempt to cross the river, either here or at some point near. I want you to take charge of the two guns just yonder."

Lieutenant Bleecker said: "General, I have had no experience in artillery, and —"

But the general mounted his horse at that moment, and was off at a gallop before the sentence was finished, saying to Captain Goodman, his adjutant-general: "Issue an order placing him in command of the section." So that within thirty minutes after reporting for duty, Bleecker was in command of a section of artillery, and with a good prospect of an engagement. He had expected, when he left the infantry service, that he would see less fighting, but this would indicate he might find work in his cavalry experience, and so subsequent events proved. Very few weeks passed during the next two years when there was no fighting. The occasion, however, was a blessing, because it took his thoughts away from home.

Very soon General Chalmers, on his rounds, drew up at the lieutenant's position, and accosted him most pleasantly, saying: "Keep your eye open, Lieutenant, and make it warm for them when they come."

The lieutenant was in love with his general from that moment. Toward evening, our scouts reported that the enemy had returned to Memphis. The lieutenant felt greatly relieved, and at once sought the general, to whom he explained his ignorance of artillery. When he reported, he wore a fatigue jacket trimmed in red, which led the general to suppose he was an artilleryman. All hands laughed at the circumstance. The general said: "The officer who should command the section is sick, and the assignment is temporary." In a few days, the lieutenant was notified that he would do duty as a member of the general's staff in future. This was pleasant news and greatly appreciated, and was quickly communicated to his dear mother, whom he knew would be much pleased to hear it.

The general's staff at that time consisted of Captain W. A. Goodman, A.A.G.; Major Andrew G. Mills, Acting Asst. Inspector-Genl.; Lieutenant George T. Banks, A.D.C.; Major Brodie S. Crump, Commissary; Captain A. D. Bright, A.A.A.G.; Captain Samuel O'Neil, Quartermaster; Colonel Casey Young, A.D.C.; and Lieutenant Julius A. Taylor, A.D.C. Captain W. H. Carroll commanded the escort company, with C.T. Smith and Clayton R. Jones as his lieutenants. This was indeed a happy and congenial circle, and Lieutenant Bleecker soon became attached to all of them. General Chalmers had formerly commanded a brigade in Bragg's army, which command distinguished itself at Shiloh, at Murfreesboro, at Perryville, and other places. The general had but recently been sent to collect all the troops in North Mississippi, and defend the prairie country from destruction by the Federals. This section supplied nearly all our corn. Chalmers' force at this time was poorly equipped, and only a small portion organized, but the general began active steps to get his organization perfected, and the men well drilled.

(The following is copied from Hancock's *History of the Second Tennessee Cavalry*):

Brigadier-General James Ronald Chalmers

J.R. Chalmers, son of the Hon. Judge Joseph W. Chalmers (who was in the United States Senate under Polk's administration), was born in Halifax county, Va., on the 11th of January, 1831. He is the oldest and only survivor of seven children – four sons and three daughters. In 1834 or 1835 he removed with his father to Jackson, Tenn., and thence to Holly Springs, Marshall county, Miss., in 1839, where he was sent to school and prepared for college, which he entered at Columbia, S.C., in September, 1848, where he graduated in December, 1851, taking the second honor in a class of about fifteen. Returning to Holly Springs, he at once entered upon the study of law in the office of Barton & Chalmers, the firm being composed of his father, and the great and gifted Roger Barton. In 1852 he was a delegate to the Democratic Convention which nominated Franklin Pierce for President. The next year he began to practice law at Holly Springs, and in 1857 he was elected district attorney of the Seventh Judicial District, over several worthy and popular competitors. He was soon recognized as one of the ablest prosecuting attorneys in the State, and greatly increased and strengthened his popularity. He was a delegate from De Soto county to the Mississippi State Convention, which passed the ordinance of secession, in January, 1861, and chairman of the Military Committee in that body.

The subject of this sketch was elected colonel of the Ninth Mississippi Regiment of infantry, which was the first that entered the Confederate service from that State. His first engagement was a successful attack upon Fort Pickens, on Santa Rosa Island, south of Pensacola, Fla.

Chalmers was appointed brigadier-general on the 13th of February, 1862, and was in command of the forces that drove Sherman and his gun-boats back from Eastport, Miss., on March the 12th, and thus saved Bear Creek Bridge from destruction, and the Memphis and Charleston Railroad from falling into the hands of the enemy. At the battle of Shiloh he commanded the extreme right brigade, and made the last charge on Sunday that was made by the Confederates on that eventful day. Balls passed through his clothing, and his horse was shot from under him on Monday. When the Confederate army fell back to Tupelo, Bragg assigned Chalmers to a cavalry command for a short time, but, having been recalled to take charge of his infantry brigade, he went with Bragg on his Kentucky campaign. The former made an unsuccessful attack upon Mumfordville, and was complimented by the latter for what he did. At the battle of Murfreesboro, General Chambers was severely wounded, and before he had fully recovered from the effect of his wound, he was assigned by Bragg to the command of the cavalry in North-western Mississippi, at the special request of the governor of that State – Pettus.

General Chalmers now went to work in his new field and organized the "squads" and companies into regiments, which afterward, under his command, formed a prominent part in that terrible column that enabled Forrest to perform his wondrous feats and made his name immortal, causing him to go down the ages as the "Wizard of the Saddle."

General Chalmers commanded the first division of Forrest's cavalry from January, 1864, to the close of the war, as set forth in the following pages of this work, to which I refer the reader for the balance of the military career of this gallant and noble officer. He accepted the terms of surrender in good faith, and returned to his home in North Mississippi, where he again began the practice of his profession – the law.

In 1872, he was on the electoral ticket in Mississippi for Horace Greeley; in 1875, he was elected to the State senate; and in 1876, he was elected to Congress from what is known as the "Shoe-string District," and again in 1878 without opposition. In 1880, he was returned as elected, but was unseated in a contest by John R. Lynch, the Republican candidate. General Chalmers then removed from Vicksburg to Sardis, Miss., and in 1882, became an independent Democratic candidate for Congress against V. H. Manning, the regular Democratic nominee, and after a close, exciting canvass, was elected.

As a speaker, General Chalmers is fluent, bold, pointed, and fearless. In his style, he draws occasionally upon a cultivated and exuberant fancy, but indulges more frequently in pointed and racy anecdote. As a friend, he is sincere, true, and devoted; as an enemy, fearless and inflexible; but at all times just and generous, as ready to atone for a wrong, when he is convinced that he has committed one, as he is, upon the other hand, steadfast and immovable when satisfied that he is right.

CHAPTER THIRTEEN

General Chalmers Organizes His Forces –
The Fight at Coldwater River – Gallant Conduct
of Colonel McCulloch – Captain Carroll Gives
McCulloch a Dining – Gallant Conduct of
Major Grant Wilson of the Federal Army

The weather had been very favorable for the past month. Every company was drilled daily, and battalion drill twice a week was the order. With the exception of the Second Missouri, Willis' Texas Battalion, the Second Arkansas, and two companies of the Seventh Tennessee, the troops were "green," composed mostly of boys under and men over military age. The boys and their horses soon acquired most of the important movements, but the old men knew no more about drill at the end of two months than at the beginning. Neither did their horses. It was really amusing to watch them. The old men could not distinguish between column right and right forward fours right. They had their horses equally confused. You could depend upon it with almost absolute certainty, when marching in line, and the command fours right was given, half of them would wheel to the left. The general, however, persevered with wonderful patience, and, by sandwiching the boys and old men, succeeded in directing the new commands very well. Before, however, the organization was complete, General Mower, with a division of infantry, cavalry, and artillery, was arranging to leave Memphis. General Chalmers was advised of his movement through Henderson's scouts, and ordered Colonel Bob McCulloch, of the Second Missouri, with his own regiment, Willis' Texas Battalion, two small pieces of artillery, and the two companies of the Seventh Tennessee, to move toward Memphis and impede the advance of Mower as best he could.

Colonel McCulloch moved from Panola direct to Como, and found that the Federals in large numbers were approaching Coldwater river. McCulloch determined to give Mower all the trouble possible while crossing the little river. He made no halt at Como, but hurried on to meet the enemy. The balance of our command was distributed along the Tallahatchie river, at Wyatt, Abbeville, and Rocky Ford, guarding the crossings. General Chalmers sent couriers with orders to those commands to cross the river at once and meet him at Como. The general, his staff, and escort company reached Como about noon, where he awaited the arrival of the troops, numbering about one thousand men all told. McCulloch had under his command about seven hundred men; total, seventeen hundred. Colonel Slemons, with the Second Arkansas, was the first to reach Como. The general moved at once with his command to the support of McCulloch. The Federals about the same time began to cross Coldwater river under cover of artillery fire. McCulloch came in view just as the first boat reached the south bank, and, though exposed to a heavy fire from artillery, dashed recklessly at them with the Second Missouri and Willis' Texas Battalion, capturing the boat and all on it. This charge astonished the enemy, but he soon recovered. Then a furious fight began across the river. General Mower made several other attempts to cross, but we defeated him in each instance.

His plans, however, had been well conceived. At the time he left Memphis with his division, via Hernando, he ordered General Hatch, with his brigade of cavalry and four pieces of artillery, to move from Collierville to cut off General Chalmers, whom he concluded would advance from Panola to meet him. The promptness and rapidity of McCulloch's movement staggered him, and caused him to pause and consider. He had not supposed he would meet any resistance farther north than Sardis. The two regiments from Abbeville and Wyatt reached us about 9 P.M., but we heard nothing from Major Alex. Chalmers, who, with four companies, had been guarding the crossing at Rocky Ford. Soon after going into camp, scouts reported that a force of two thousand cavalry, under General Hatch, was encamped six miles to the east of us. These troops had heard the cannonading in the evening, and expected to reach our rear early the following morning. At daylight we were in the saddle. General Hatch had a large force, much better equipped, almost in our rear, and General Mower a division in our front. Our future status was exceedingly uncertain, but the troops depended on General Chalmers, and he brought them around safely. When the command had mounted, the general moved south toward Como until we reached a woods. Passing through to the east, we came into the road by which Hatch was moving just as his column had passed by, so that instead of Hatch gaining our rear we were in his, and ready to give him a brush. The men felt better and the troops were anxious to try conclusions. Immediately Major Chalmers, with his battalion, came in sight, and we were equally glad to see each other. He explained to the general that soon after leaving Rocky Ford he met Hatch, who cut him off from a direct route to Como, and he decided to dog his rear rather than incur the delay of a long ride to the south. He captured a number of men and horses. General Chalmers determined to attack Hatch, and ordered Major Chal-mers to press him, which he did with considerable success, capturing a large number of Negroes, mules, and cattle, which Hatch had taken from the people along his line of march. Hatch would make no fight, but retreated to the Memphis and Charleston Railroad. Mower returned to Memphis via Hernando. Reaching the latter, they set fire to every vacant house and all public buildings in the town. The place was nearly destroyed.

    Hernando was General Chalmers' home, and his wife was then living there. Mrs. Chalmers at that time was in ill-health, and being notified that her house would be fired, she sent for the officer who gave the information, and apprised him of her helpless condition. He stated he had no discretion in the matter; she must get out. She asked if there was an officer near who had authority, but received no satisfactory reply. Her faithful Negro servant determined to save the house if possible, and went out begging the Federal officers wherever she found them to spare her mistress the house. Finally, Major Grant Wilson heard her pleadings, rode to the house, and drove every rascal away. He ordered a guard to protect the property, and tendered his services to Mrs. Chalmers in any capacity desired. Major Wilson, of course, won the undying gratitude and respect of Mrs. Chalmers, and placed the general under an obligation which he can never fully repay. General Chalmers wrote him a letter thanking him for his consideration, and received a reply stating that there was no obligation – he was not in the service to burn houses and make war on helpless women.

Major Wilson afterward became General Wilson. During one of General Chalmers' terms in Congress he had the pleasure of meeting him again, when a very warm friendship was formed, and continues to this day. General Wilson is now an Episcopal clergyman.

This little fight at Coldwater was a brilliant affair. General Chalmers, with about twelve hundred men and two pieces of inferior artillery, defeated a well-equipped army of not less than five thousand men and twelve pieces of artillery, forcing them back to Memphis. Two companies were sent to follow the enemy and keep posted on his movements. General Chalmers in a few days went into camp at Como with the entire force. This was about the last of July, 1863.

Colonel Monroe Wallace, with a large number of his Negroes, horses, mules, etc., had left his beautiful home near Como to seek a place of safety in Georgia or in South Carolina, his native State. He had personally returned to look after his affairs, and when we went into camp at Como he invited General Chalmers to occupy his house as his headquarters. It was a lovely home, beautifully furnished, the beds supplied with snowy linen sheets and soft lamb's wool blankets, big, fat, feather pillows and bolsters, the smoke house was well stocked with home cured meat, and a large drove of fine fat turkeys roamed the lot. All of these the colonel told us to enjoy. There was no string to the invitation. Colonel Wallace belonged to that class of Southern gentleman who dispensed true hospitality. His manner was courtly, and his attentions were pleasing without being effusive. He had been educated in the school of polite and cultivated society. If it was necessary to give up his carriage horses, he would surrender them gracefully, and, to all appearances, willingly. He was a typical Southerner. He bade us good-bye, and left his old cook, "Aunt Jenny," and his body servant, "Uncle Steve," with instructions to do the best they could for us. We had turkey and lye hominy, ham and fat biscuits, sweet potatoes and butter. We had turkey hash every morning, though there was not a scrap of turkey left from dinner. Several days were passed like a dream. The party embraced the general and his entire staff, heretofore named, and Captain W. H. Carroll, commanding the escort.

Frequent discussions were had about the gallant little fight at Coldwater. Captain Carroll said General Chalmers had a habit of going into places where it was terribly hot, and, furthermore, seemed never to be entirely satisfied unless his (Carroll's) company was in the hottest places on the line. He argued with great earnestness and said he thought an escort company should be held more as a reserve. General Chalmers entered into our discussions on perfect equality with the others, and was without doubt among the most courteous as well as the most companionable of men. He wanted nothing which he could not divide with his staff, and he treated them as his equals in every particular. Carroll contended that the charge on the enemy at Coldwater, made by Colonel McCulloch, with the Second Missouri, was the most gallant he ever saw, and he proposed to emphasize his opinion by inviting Colonel McCulloch to a dining at our house. He rode over to McCulloch's headquarters, and extended the invitation. The day was set, and Aunt Jenny and Uncle Steve were told of the importance of having the dinner up to the standard. After Aunt Jenny signified her understanding, Carroll discussed the occasion with the general and members of the staff, except Captain Bright and Lieutenant Bleecker, whom he missed, probably on account of an oversight. He referred to it as a banquet, worthy to be compared to the feasts which in the olden times were spread before the kings. His whole soul was occupied in the work. He had undertaken to show honors to a deserving and distinguished officer.

The day before the dinner was to come off, Captain Bright inquired of Lieutenant Bleecker if he had been invited to Carroll's dinner. The lieutenant replied in the negative. Bright said: "Keep perfectly quiet, and I will secure you an invitation. I understand it will be a conspicuous occasion, and you must be there."

The day arrived. The general and his staff made their toilets with more than ordinary care. It was an ideal day, one of those glorious balmy days, laden with autumn's rich content, and the air was perfumed with delightful odors. The world smiled on Carroll, and he was in a gay and happy mood. As soon as breakfast was over, he sought Aunt Jenny, to inquire about the preparations.

She said: "Lord, Mister Carroll, I aynt gwine cook no big dinner."

Carroll was shocked and stunned, and demanded an explanation. Aunt Jenny told him that "Mister Bright dun got a letter from marster, an', an' he said he dun change he mind, he dun give the house over to Mr. Bright, cluden' of the turkeys, the hams, the coffee, and every thing, and, furthestmore, Mr. Bright dun told me not to kill no more of his turkeys, ner bile no more of his hams, and Ise gwine to mind my marster, ceptin' God doan spare me."

Bright saw Carroll talking to Aunt Jenny, and walked down to the stables so that Carroll could not find him. Carroll soon had all the army niggers hunting for him. It was a serious situation. He had talked so confidently of his ability to make the day pleasant; he would preside and do the honors, etc., but the hour of despair had arrived. Finally, Bright was found; Carroll poured out great volumes of invectives at him; it came forth like smoke out of a chimney. Bright took it calmly, and after Carroll had exhausted his cauldron of sulphur and fire, quietly asked: "What on the earth is the matter with you, Bill?" He pretended to know nothing of the intended compliment to Colonel McCulloch.

Carroll replied: "We have talked about nothing else for a

week."

Bright said: "You have not talked to Lieutenant Bleecker nor me."

Then it dawned on Carroll, and he extended to both the most pressing invitation to be present. Bright gave Aunt Jenny permission to kill the turkey and cook every thing else desired to make the dinner worthy of the guest.

Then, addressing Carroll, Bright began to quote him Scripture. He said: "Bill, Joshua attempted the unreasonable, and the walls of Jericho fell down; Abraham and David attempted unreasonable things, and they failed, too; you can not expect to leave Bleecker and me out when the dinner bell rings; that would be unreasonable."

It is sufficient to say that the dinner was a success, and none enjoyed it more than Bright. Carroll began at once to plan for revenge, and he got it, as we will explain further on.

CHAPTER FOURTEEN

The Men Taught How to Jerk Beef – Colonel Young and "The Colt" – Gallant Conduct of Major Chalmers – Narrow Escape of General Sherman

General Chalmers moved to the south bank of the Tallahatchie, and made his headquarters at Moss' Mill. He was advised by Henderson's scouts that troops were moving from Memphis to reinforce the Federal army at Chattanooga. He determined to cut the Memphis and Charleston Railroad at several points, and began getting his command in readiness. Our commissary was confined to meal and beef; there was no bacon to be had, so the general decided to send his men to cooking school to learn how to cure beef. Willis' Texas Battalion, some two hundred men, were experts in the art of curing beef, as well as in charging the enemy. The general requested Colonel Willis to detail a number of his men to go among the other commands and teach them how to jerk beef. A day was devoted to the work with success.

The men soon caught the idea and saw the benefits, and for the remainder of the war, wherever General Chalmers' division camped, forks and poles could be seen with little dabs of beef hanging on them over a smoke. Oftentimes dried beef proved a boon to our men. It could be carried for days and weeks, and did not require cooking. The writer remembers on many occasions seeing the men while on the march munching the jerked beef without bread, joking each other, and inviting citizens along the route to "come in and have dinner, etc." On one occasion we were on the march through a sparcely settled country, where it was impossible to get any thing. The general and his staff camped under a big oak the previous evening without supper, and departed in the morning without breakfast. We rode along silent as the grave, except the patter, patter of the horses' feet, and the rattle of the spurs and sabers. The escort company followed, but they were as gay as red birds in spring. They carried in their saddle pockets good sized "hunks" of jerked beef. The sallies and jests of the boys did not improve the situation. We felt no better, because of their being happy. We rode forward in silence; not a word was spoken.

Finally, we overtook the Second Missouri. Lieutenant Dick Eubanks rode at the head of his company. As we passed, Eubanks said: "General, stop and eat breakfast with me."

The general turned his horse quick as thought and rode back to him, said: "Ah! Lieutenant, you please me greatly," at the same time reaching for Eubanks' hunk of beef, which was given with apparent liberal hospitality. But, as the general rode off, Eubanks exclaimed in a low tone: "May the saints forgive me! Did you ever see a fellow lose three days rations so easily as that?"

This remark of Dick Eubanks, who was a splendid specimen of Southern manhood, as well as a brave and devoted soldier, brought forth a great laugh.

While in camp at Moss' Mill, the headquarters "niggers" were told to get every thing in readiness, and be certain to have a supply of jerked beef well salted. We had quite a number of them. Wallace belonged to the general, Hage to Lieutenant Banks, Boston to Major Mills, George to Major Chalmers, Jim and Burton to Lieutenant Bleecker, and Uncle Bedney to Colonel Young. Uncle Bedney, George and Jim were very religious, while Wallace, Burton, Hage and Boston were not. Jim was our cook. He had authority to detail either of the others to assist him whenever he needed an assistant, and he complained that, since reaching Moss' Mill, he could get neither Wallace, Burton, Hage, nor Boston. They were called up and asked about it. Each said they were busy getting the horses in good condition and polishing the spurs, sabers, etc. The following morning the general ordered Lieutenant Bleecker to see each colonel during the day, requesting them to meet at his headquarters for advice. He called on Uncle Bedney to go down to the stable and to tell Burton to bring out his horse. Uncle Bedney said: "Dat horse aynt fitten to travel, he aynt been fed yit," and on being asked why, replied: "dem niggers aynt cum home yit."

Lieutenant Bleecker walked down to the stable and found, as stated by Uncle Bedney, that the horses had not been fed. But he heard quarreling going on up in the loft. He climbed up the ladder, and found them in a game of seven-up, which they had been playing all night by a dim tallow candle. It did not take long to close the game after Bleecker found them. Going back to camp, he told the story.

Uncle Bedney said, "I knowed it, I knowed it, I dun told em day would sho git ketched."

Major Chalmers asked Uncle Bedney why he had not reported on the niggers. Said: "Oh, Mars Ham, it's bad luck, it's bad luck to port on folks playing cards. Deed 'tis, sir! deed 'tis, sir!" Colonel Young, Uncle Bedney's master, had been absent for two weeks on leave, and returned while we camped at the mill. He brought a new horse with him. (Now this is a true story.) He was the largest horse we ever saw. The writer has traveled from Halifax, Nova Scotia, to Palm Beach, Florida, since that time; he has drank water from the source of the San Antonia, and has seen thousands of horses, but not one of them approached in size the one Colonel Young rode into camp at Moss' Mill. The colonel said he was a colt, and always referred to him as "the colt." He was a strawberry roan. The writer was at that time but a boy, and the impressions made upon the mind at his then age are different from those made on the mind of a maturer person, but his recollection of the colt is, that he was as high as the second story of the mill, and at this day, thirty-two years since that time, he can not change the opinion. The day after Colonel Young reached the mill, we were guessing on the colt's height. Boston, on being asked for his opinion, said, "I nose, I dun measure him. He's thirty-five foot high." Uncle Bedney would lead him alongside of a tree, and then climb the tree in order to curry his back. We never found a stable door or a gin-house high enough for him to get under during the war. Whenever we broke camp, we left Colonel Young behind trying to mount the colt. If there was not a high fence about, he would lead him until he found a sapling which he could climb; but, after he once mounted, he had no trouble keeping up, for the colt could walk as fast as the other horses could trot.

A few weeks before we camped at Moss' Mill, a man reported to General Chalmers offering his services as a spy. He had good references from several Confederate generals, including General Price. He claimed that he would be able to enter the enemy's lines at will, having a paper from General Hurlbut passing him at all times. He made several trips into Memphis, but the information he brought amounted to nothing. He gave his name as Pearson. General Chalmers was suspicious of him, and decided to deceive him as to the point he intended to attack on the Memphis and Charleston Railroad. He therefore told him that he would move against Corinth.

"Why," said Pearson, "it would be impossible to take Corinth with your force."

"But," said the general, "I am only supposed to cover General Loring's division of infantry; he is moving on Corinth from Mobile, and we can defeat any force which can be moved there from the near garrisons."

Pearson left us with this information on his mind, and on September 7th, we marched toward Holly Springs. Arriving there, we spent the night, and the following day moved toward La Grange, which was in the direction of Corinth. Pearson had ample time to advise General Hurlbut, which he did, as events proved. General Chalmers' force consisted of the Second Missouri, Willis' Texas Battalion, Seventh Tennessee, Third Mississippi, Second Arkansas, Major A.H. Chalmers' Mississippi Battalion, and two small pieces of artillery, about 1,600 men all told.

Just before we reached Salem, the scouts reported a strong cavalry force at that place. It was evident the enemy believed General Chalmers was moving on to Corinth, and the force was sent to meet him. This Federal force consisted of five regiments of cavalry and two batteries of artillery, all under command of Colonel Crellis, and numbered three thousand men, according to Colonel Crellis' own statement. There were two roads leading to Salem, one from Grand Junction, and the other from Holly Springs, which converged at the foot of the hill before reaching the little town. We approached by the road from Holly Springs. The angle formed by the convergence of the roads was covered with woods. Major Chalmers was ordered to bring on the fight. His battalion of six companies rested near the intersection of the roads. The enemy's guns were making the woods rattle. Lieutenant Bleecker carried the order to Major Chalmers, and saw his men advance. The horses were left in the woods, and the men took their places in line. Major Chalmers was riding a very pretty bay horse, and as he passed along, gave the order, "Forward!" Just at that moment a shell exploded immediately in front of the line, killing the color bearer, the flag falling to the ground. Major Chalmers rode to the colors, and, leaning down without dismounting, caught them up. Most of his men had seen very little service; a majority of them were boys under eighteen. The shell, therefore, created some confusion among them, but when the major waived the flag above his head, and called on them to follow, they gave a yell and rallied to the colors. Major Chalmers was by nature a handsome man, but he was a picture for an artist as he rode the little bay up the hill facing the enemy's lines, with that flag above him. Shot and shell filled the air with shrieks and other wicked sounds, but they did not check the boys. Nothing could stop them as long as the major waved the flag.

The general, seeing the rush of the Mississippi boys, moved the command rapidly to their support, and within five minutes the entire force was engaged. Salem was, and is yet, only a small country village, but things were lively there that day. A few minutes after the two lines met face to face, Colonel McCulloch, with the Second Missouri and Seventh Tennessee, mounted, sought the enemy's flank. The general had strong hopes of capturing a good part of them, but, before McCulloch could gain the rear, they fell back, mounted their horses, and left us in possession of their dead and wounded. Night came on, and the pursuit was abandoned. A detail was left to bury the dead and care for the wounded of both sides, and we rode rapidly back to Holly Springs. As General Chalmers believed, Pearson was a Yankee spy; he gave General Hurlbut information that Chalmers would attack Corinth. As proof of this, reinforcements were sent to Corinth. We remained a few hours at Holly Springs, then marched to Collierville. Major Mitchell, with two companies of Major Chalmers' battalion, was sent to cut the railroad east of Collierville, and Major Cousins, of the Second Missouri, with two companies, was ordered to do the same on the west side, to prevent any reinforcements from reaching the garrison. We arrived within two miles of the station about daylight. Our advance guard captured the Yankee outpost, and, as soon as the prisoners were turned over, made a dash at the inner guards, who, however, discovered our men in time to escape and give the alarm. We moved forward at a gallop. Colonel McGuirk, with the Third Mississippi, was ordered to go in the rear of the fort, and attack from that point, while the balance of the command would advance from the south. McGuirk reached his place promptly, and found that the two Illinois regiments, Seventh and Eighth, had gone, leaving a lot of dismounted men in camp. These dismounted men, about one hundred, ran in every direction. It was just after daylight, and the attack was a perfect surprise to them. Some of McGuirk's men began to chase the fugitives on foot, while others dismounted and began to go through the tents. General Chalmers' plan was for McGuirk to charge the rear of the fort simultaneously with his attack in front. We formed line, and moved through the woods to a point about four hundred yards from the fort, and waited for McGuirk. Our skirmish line was hotly engaged; the enemy, using artillery, threw shells high above and beyond us. General Chalmers, growing impatient, sent Lieutenant Banks to order the Third Mississippi to the attack. A moment afterward, a long train of freight cars rolled into the station from Memphis, from which the Thirteenth Regulars disembarked and ran into the fort. We knew, of course, that Major Cousins had failed to cut the road on the west, as ordered, otherwise the train could not have passed him. General Chalmers knew that any further delay would be ruinous, and, therefore, gave the order to charge. Our men moved forward in fine style, but were met by a hot fire. They charged within about sixty yards of the fort. We could see nothing of the enemy except the tops of their heads. General Chalmers saw it would be a great sacrifice to storm the fort, and, therefore, withdrew under cover of the woods, the enemy in the meantime shelling our position sharply.

General Chalmers' plans were well laid, and had McGuirk charged the fort before the arrival of the Thirteenth Regulars, instead of halting in the cavalry camp, the garrison would, unquestionably, have been captured. Or had Major Cousins cut the road, as ordered, the Thirteenth Regulars could not have reinforced the garrison, and in that event we would have captured it. After the line had fallen back, and was resting in the woods, Lieutenant Bleecker was sent to find Lieutenant Banks and Colonel McGuirk. Arriving at the point where the rear of the train rested, he noticed a number of our men in the cars throwing out saddles, bridles, blankets, and bundles. Bleecker dismounted, hitched his horse to a telegraph pole, and boarded the coach at the end of the train. He wanted some of the plunder. The coach was empty, but on the seat was a handsome sword, which he picked up. He ran out to where the men were busy getting saddles. In one of the cars were several horses. It had not occurred to the men that the horses could be gotten out. Bleecker said, "Make them jump out," and with that he pulled himself into the car, untied a fine horse, and led him to the door. After much urging the horse jumped out. It did not require much time for the boys to get the others out. With their plunder, they all galloped off to catch the command, which had retired about a mile back, where the general waited in vain for the Federals to follow. Through the baggage taken from the cars, we discovered that General Sherman and staff were passengers on the train. We captured all their personal baggage. The sword which Bleecker found had the name of "Lieut. Col.-Ewing, Gen. Sherman's Staff," on the cover. It was a very handsome one. The horse which Bleecker captured was also a fine animal, and most likely was the one ridden by General Sherman. Bleecker was very proud of his horse, but his pride of ownership was short lived, for the general ordered the quartermaster to take charge of him, as well as the others captured.

As soon as we ascertained that General Sherman was in the fort, the failure was doubly regretted. Barton, one of Lieutenant Bleecker's Negroes, named the captured horse, "Sherman," and often said his "marster captured Old Sherman."

Think of the circumstances which make or destroy the reputation or success of a man! Had McGuirk moved on and captured the fort, instead of allowing his men to halt in camp, or had Major Cousins cut the road as ordered, Sherman would almost certainly have been captured, and the story of the burning of churches, convents, and school-houses, and the destruction of every thing to eat along his line of march in Georgia, without a foe in his front, would never have been told, and future generations would not have read how helpless women, often sick and destitute, appealed to him to spare their houses and a few rations of meal, and how contemptuously they were pushed aside. The houses were burned as well as all their provisions. Had we captured Sherman, he never would have had the opportunity to make himself famous, and in all probability he would have been in prison during the balance of the war.

We fell back, going south, and crossed the Coldwater at Ingraham's Mill.

CHAPTER FIFTEEN

Fight at Moscow, Tennessee – Bright Pays
His Respects to Carroll – A Yankee Cavalryman
Kills "Uncle Steve" – A Texan Lassoes a Woman

On the last of November, 1863, General Chalmers received advice from General S. D. Lee that General Forrest, with a small force, would cross the Memphis and Charleston Railroad and go into West Tennessee, and desiring him to assist Forrest through. We moved south, crossing the Tallahatchie at Panola. Orders were issued for four days' rations, and every thing was put in readiness for a quick movement. It had been raining very hard for two days. We crossed the river at Rocky Ford, and moved in the direction of Grand Junction, to co-operate with General Lee, who left Okalona with Furguson's and Ross' brigades about the same time. General Chalmers advanced on La Grange, driving in the enemy's pickets, and threatening the garrison, while Furguson and Ross were gathering around Pocahontas. These demonstrations were intended to attract the attention of the enemy, and prevent his interference with the passage of General Forrest into West Tennessee. It was General Forrest's purpose to enlist all the men he could find, who were at that time within the enemy's lines. There were numbers who had been wounded and allowed to go home, but who, after getting well, made no effort to rejoin their commands. These men belonged to the Army of Tennessee principally. It was a desperate undertaking, but Forrest boldly marched into the enemy's lines with about three hundred and fifty men, crossing the railroad at Saulsbury. He remained at Jackson nearly a month, surrounded by about forty thousand of the enemy. After the passage, General S.D. Lee, who was in command of all the cavalry in the State, decided to make further demonstrations against the garrisons along the Memphis and Charleston Railroad. This would prevent pursuit of Forrest. Early on the morning of December 4th, he moved with all the command toward Moscow, General Chalmers, with McCulloch's brigade, taking the advance. Arriving at that point, General Lee directed that McCulloch should attack from the south on the public road leading to Moscow (this road crossed Wolf river), and Ross was ordered to capture and destroy the railroad bridge west of Moscow. Chalmers, McCulloch, Ross, and Lee discussed the plan for a few minutes, when General Lee said: "Colonel Ross, take the bridge. I give you this opportunity to win your spurs" (meaning, of course, a brigadiership). Ross dashed off, and in a short while was hotly engaged. McCulloch was not pleased with the remark. His commission as colonel was older than that of Ross, and he felt that the sentiment was an injustice to him. He left Missouri with his regiment, and had made a brilliant reputation. He had fought all over the territory as far south as Grenada, neither his men nor himself ever failing to do their duty. As he rode off to make the attack as directed, he remarked: "He has a chance to win his spurs, but he won't do it to-day. He won't burn the bridge."

McCulloch's brigade consisted of the Second Missouri, Willis' Texas Battalion, Seventh Tennessee, Major Chalmers' battalion, and Hovis' and Wisdom's regiments. McCulloch was known as "Colonel Black Bob." The lieutenant-colonel of the Second Missouri was also named Robert McCulloch. They were cousins. The colonel had dark hair and beard, while the lieutenant-colonel had red hair and beard, and they were known as "Colonel Black Bob" and "Colonel Red Bob." Nor was there in the Confederate army two men whose services were given more entirely to the cause. They had dash and daring, and they had the bravery of Forrest, yet they were modest almost to a fault. Colonel Black Bob quickly formed his line, and advanced through the river bottom, driving in the enemy's skirmishers. The roadway was considerably higher than the ground on either side, having been raised from time to time on account of overflow. Behind the earth embankment the enemy formed a line, securing a great advantage. McCulloch led his men, dismounted, and moved through the cypress knees and slush, driving the foe from this favored position. He had no hope of winning spurs, but governed by that principle which controlled him at all times, he determined to do his duty. The fight was furious. The enemy's shell and grape-shot shattered trees and threw bark and limbs on all sides. As soon as McCulloch dislodged the enemy from behind the road-bed, their guns swept it. But with that gallantry which always characterized his men, they pushed on, driving the enemy to the river. As the last of them were crossing the bridge on their retreat, some of McCulloch's men mixed with them in a hand-to-hand fight. McCulloch lost many good men, among whom was his adjutant, Captain Gaines, a gallant and heroic officer.

In the meantime, Ross had been hotly engaged at the trestle on the railroad, but did not make any impression. He was forced to retire without burning the bridge. McCulloch established his line as instructed, but on account of Ross' failure, was ordered to fall back. We moved south to Panola, and the command was distributed along the river at various crossings.

While the fight at Moscow was not a success, it accomplished the object of getting General Forrest through the lines, and left the enemy in doubt about future movements. We had no other troops engaged at Moscow, except Ross' and McCulloch's brigades. After the fight Furguson was sent back to the Mobile and Ohio Railroad. General Chalmers, with his staff and escort, were on the left of McCulloch's line during the fight, where he could watch both positions. His staff officers were going constantly with orders and reporting back to him the situation at different points during the engagement. He found occasion to send Captain Carroll, of the escort company, with an order to Colonel McCulloch, "To drive the enemy from the road." Things were boiling in that cypress swamp about that time. As Carroll returned, he noticed Captain Tom Henderson, of the scouts, sitting on his roan behind three large Tupelo gums, which were near each other, watching the enemy's line. Grape and cannister were playing inharmonious tunes among the trees. Carroll was no doubt praying for, as well as seeking, a place of safety as he rushed through the woods, for he knew he must go at least a quarter before he was out of range. Seeing Captain Henderson he turned his course toward him, and sought the partial shelter of the trees. Captain Bright soon afterward was sent by the general to order Colonel Hovis with his regiment to the left, to meet a movement from the enemy which was intended to flank our position. Bright rode from the opposite direction, of course, and saw Carroll and Captain Henderson. He went dashing through the shot and shell with bated breath, and the chances were very much in favor of his never getting back. There were no accident insurance companies in those days. Bright was a remarkable man, well named, and full of fun; his presence invariably inspired any crowd he was with. He was jovial and companionable, as bright as a new dollar, and never had the blues so far as we knew, and, above all, he was a man of resources. He had a good memory, and an eye for "the eternal fitness of things." He drew rein, and said: "Bill, General Lee directs that you find Colonel Hovis quickly, and order him to take his regiment to the left of Colonel McCulloch's line, to meet a flank movement of the Yankees; he, also, desires you to accompany the regiment on the movement." There was no time to parley. Carroll dashed off through the woods like a rabbit running from a burning sedge field. Just before reaching Colonel Hovis, who was on the right, he saw Captain Gaines galloping in the same direction. They bore toward each other, but just as they were about to meet Captain Gaines was shot through with an ounce ball and fell. In a moment the riderless horse was killed also. Carroll soon reached Colonel Hovis, and together, the two at the head of the column, moved to the rear and around to the left. General Chalmers with the escort company was hotly engaged with the enemy when they reached him. Carroll joined his company. The intended flank movement was balked.

That night, while we sat around the big wood fire, each had his story to tell of the dangers he had passed through, and all paid compliments to the gallant fellows of McCulloch's brigade.

Bright listened to Carroll as he went over the events of the day, after which he related how he sent Carroll on the dangerous mission. We laughed at the circumstance, and all agreed that Bright was the smartest man in the party. Carroll took in every word. He sat silently, and seemed to be dreaming. Finally, he asked Bright: "Is that a fact? Didn't General Lee send that order? Great Heavens! Suppose I had been killed!" He got up from his seat on the log and walked over to Bright. Bright had the most exasperating laugh, and he was giving it to Carroll for all it was worth.

Addressing him, Carroll said: "I do not mind doing your work, but I have got all I want of that d—n laugh."

Bright replied: "Bill, you remember that dinner you gave to McCulloch?"

We remained on the south bank of the Tallahatchie until December the 18th, when we crossed again and moved in the direction of Memphis. The move was intended to prevent the enemy from sending any troops after General Forrest. We reached Como on the 20th, and made headquarters again at Colonel Wallace's. We reached there at night, and found every thing in confusion. Aunt Jenny opened the house and did every thing in her power to make us comfortable, but sad scenes had been enacted since our last visit. The place looked very much as if a cyclone had struck it. Aunt Jenny's smiles and hospitable manner had gone; she told us the story between sobs.

She said: "They killed poor Steve; them hateful Yankees killed him. Soon as you all left marster's house, they come galloping all around 'bout the place, shooting our calves and hogs and chickens, and every thing they could see. They rode their horses over mistis' flowers, and dun every thing they could that was mean. After they dun all this meanness, they began to cuss Steve and me. Steve told them they did not have any manners; that marster didn't have nary nigger but what was better raised than them. Seem like they got madder at Steve. They told him to draw water for their horses. Steve didn't want to do it, but he said marster told him to be polite to every body when they come to the house, and he went to draw the water. I am telling you the truth. Them hateful Yankees come here to kill Steve. They called him a d—n rebel nigger. When he samely draw the water up, they took the bucket and dashed it on Steve; that made the old man mad, and he 'lowed marster never had cussed him, neither had he 'bused him, and they might kill him, but he won't draw no more water, and Steve didn't nuther, 'cause them hateful Yankees beat his brains out with their guns, and I'm telling you the truth, they left him lying in his blood in the mud. Then they got on their horses and galloped around, shooting bullets in the house – you see the holes in the walls yourselfs. They said the next time the rebels come to marster's house, they was going to burn it. There was nobody on the place but me, and I say to myself, what is marster going to say when he hears them hateful Yankees killed Steve. Yes, sir, we buried him, but it was nearly night before any body come along to pick Steve up. Mr. Merriwether said, 'Bury him in the garden,' so marster could see his grave when he come home. I dread for marster to come home; he 'pended mightily on Steve; he fairly loved him. I know what mistis will do. Mistis sho will grieve. She begged marster to take Steve away."

Aunt Jenny told her story without pausing to catch her breath. It was all like one sentence, and when she could say no more, being overcome with grief, she covered her face with her apron and left the house. We were a sad party; we felt that Uncle Steve had lost his life because of his attentions to us.

We remained at Como until the day before Christmas, when we moved around Memphis toward Germantown. General Chalmers had been advised that General Forrest, with a large lot of cattle and horses, would attempt to return to our lines. He recruited about a thousand men, whom he was bringing out also, but none of them had guns. General Forrest crossed near Mount Pleasant, and reached us safely with all his supplies. We returned to Como, reaching there Friday, January 1, 1864, the coldest day ever known in the country; the entire command, including the artillery, crossed creeks on ice. Our troops suffered greatly, and numbers were unable to dismount when we reached Como.

When Colonel McCulloch moved from Panola, he had considerable difficulty in getting his men across the Tallahatchie river. The crossing was accomplished on a pontoon bridge, and

A Texan Makes Use of His Lasso

only a few men and their horses could cross at a time. Those in the rear, while waiting, would slip back into the little town. General Chalmers, seeing this, sent his staff officers to order the men in line. They rode along calling on the men to close up. Several Texans, hearing the order, dashed along the street at break-neck speed; one fellow, some distance in the rear, yelling as he ran, whirling his lasso above his head, passed an old store in which stood a figure of a woman, a wire frame used for displaying cloaks and dresses. There was an old faded pink shirt on the figure, which stood near a window, the sash was out, the Texan saw it, and quick as a flash his rope caught the dummy. Down the street he flew, dragging the thing after him. It was light, and sometimes would rise six feet above the ground. Every person who saw it thought he had lassoed a woman. People looked on in dread. The fellow yelling every jump, and wearing his big hat on the back of his head, the scene was startling. Arriving at the river, he halted, drew in his rope, caught the figure under his arm, and calmly and quietly rode on the bridge, A great crowd followed to see the outcome, and when they saw what he had, a cheer went up.

Lieutenant-General N. B. Forrest

Nathan Bedford Forrest, was born on the 13th day of July, A.D. 1821, at Chapel Hill, in what was then Bedford, but is now Marshall, county, Tennessee.

His father was William Forrest, and his mother Mariam Beck, whose first-born were twins, one of whom was Nathan Bedford, the other a girl. William Forrest was the son of Nathan Forrest and Miss Baugh. Nathan Forrest was the son of Shadrack Forrest, who was of English descent, and who emigrated from the Colony of Virginia, in 1730, to Orange county, Colony of North Carolina, and in 1806 to Tennessee. Miss Baugh was of Irish origin. Mariam Beck, the wife of William Forrest, was of Scotch-Irish descent.

It will therefore be seen that Nathan Bedford was of Eng-

Lieut.-General Nathan Bedford Forrest

"Natura lo fece, e poi ruppe la stampa."

lish, Scotch, and Irish descent. William Forrest died in 1837, leaving a family of seven boys and three girls, and four months after his death the eighth son, Jeffrey, was born. The untimely death of his father deprived Nathan Bedford of any further school advantages, because his labor was necessary for the support of his mother and her children. He went to work on the little farm with all the energy and determination which characterized him afterward, and by 1849, when he was nineteen years old, had accumulated a reasonable competency for his mother and family.

In 1841, he joined a company to go to Texas, but on reaching New Orleans the necessary arrangements could not be made for the trip beyond, and the company was disbanded. Bedford and a few others determined to go on, and went so far as Houston, but, finding no demand for his services, he returned to his home in the fall of 1842.

His early life was a series of hardships, and he had many dangerous personal encounters, in all of which he acquitted himself with credit. In 1845, in the 25th year of his age, he married Miss Mary Ann Montgomery, and lived at Hernando, Miss., until 1852, when he moved to Memphis and engaged in the real estate business. He prospered, and in 1860 owned two fine plantations in Coahoma county, Miss. He enlisted as a private in Captain J. S. White's cavalry company, June 10, 1861, and in July was commissioned by the governor of Tennessee to raise a regiment of cavalry, which he armed and equipped at his own expense. From colonel he was successively promoted to brigadier-general, major-general, and lieutenant-general. Mariam Beck, the mother of General Forrest, was a woman of remarkable character, as well as great physical force, and her children undoubtedly inherited their energy and determination from her. Of the union between General Forrest and Mary Ann Montgomery, there was born one son, Wm. Montgomery Forrest, who served as captain and aide-de-camp to his father during the war.

No one was at any time during the war near the person of General Forrest, will consider the following a panegyric, nor any thing more than a just and fair delineation of the man, the soldier, and the general. It came into my possession credited to Colonel

Joyce. Who he was, and whether living or dead, I know not, and never knew. It attracted my attention and challenged my admiration when I first read it, and I give it here *verbatim*:

> Forrest was a magnetic man, standing stalwart and erect, six feet one inch, broad shouldered, long arms, high round forehead, dark gray eyes, a prominent nose, emphatic jaw, compressed lips, and a moustache setting off a face that said to all the world: "Out of my way, I'm coming."
>
> His step was firm, action impulsive, voice sonorous, and, taken all in all, there was not a soldier of the Confederacy that acted with more celerity or effective force from the 14th of June, 1861, when he became a private at Memphis, to the pth day of May, 1865, at Gainesville, Ala., where he surrendered as lieutenant-general to the United States authorities.
>
> To determine with Forrest, was to act, and the flash of his saber at the head of his columns charging the cavalry or infantry of the enemy, inspired his troops with the sunlight of victory, and they dashed into battle like the audacious warriors of Napoleon on the field of Austerlitz.
>
> The most heroic thing ever done by Forrest,[1] was his rescue of young Abel, who had killed a friend in a family quarrel, from the hands of a Memphis mob of 3,000 infuriated men. They had dragged the boy from the jail, swung the rope around his neck, and were in the act of hoisting him over a beam, when this intrepid citizen rushed through the frantic crowd, drew his bowie-knife, cut the rope, and hurried the intended victim back to jail, where the mob followed, and still demanded blood.
>
> Forrest jumped upon the jail steps, drew a revolver, and swore he would kill the first man that attempted to enter, and then and there, that lone hero, with truth and law on his side, conquered a howling, desperate mob. There was nothing in his subsequent career that equaled this for desperate, sublime courage, such as "Winkelried" displayed, when he threw himself on the Austrian spears, or Leonidas blocking the pass of Thermopylae with his immortal three hundred.

---

1. This actually occurred in Memphis in 1857, and there are men now living who witnessed the occurrence.

CHAPTER SIXTEEN

Forrest Cavalry Organized at Como, Miss. –
Seventeen Men Ordered to be Shot at Oxford –
The Battle of Okoluna – Colonel Jeffrey Forrest Killed –
A Touching Scene – The Enemy Burn Private Property

Soon after General Chalmers' command had well settled in camp, General Forrest reached us with his force, including the men he recruited in West Tennessee. He organized what proved to be the most remarkable command in the army. At that time, January 4, 1864, General Polk was assigned to the command of the department. General Forrest was given command of all the cavalry in Mississippi and North Alabama. Two brigades composed General Chalmers' division. One brigade, commanded by Colonel Robert McCulloch, consisted of the Second Missouri, Lieutenant-Colonel McCulloch; Willis' Texas Battalion, Lieutenant-Colonel Theo. Willis; Falkner's Kentucky Regiment, Colonel W.W. Falkner; Eighteenth Mississippi Regiment, Colonel A.H. Chalmers; and Keiser's Mississippi Battalion.

The second brigade, commanded by Colonel Jeffrey Forrest, was: McDonald's Battalion, Colonel Kelly; Seventh Tennessee, Colonel Duckworth; Third Mississippi, Colonel McGuirk; Fifth Mississippi, Lieutenant-Colonel Barksdale; and the Nineteenth Mississippi, Colonel Duff.

A brigade commanded by Colonel Richardson, and another by Colonel Barteau, were also organized. Within a few days, General Forrest left us for Meridian, to consult with General Polk. General Chalmers was left in command.

We moved to the south bank of the Tallahatchie, and on the morning of January 8, 1864, Henderson's scouts reported that a large force would leave Memphis about the 11th, in three columns, one via Hernando, one via Holly Springs, and the third in the direction of Okolona. Also, that Sherman, with a large force, would leave Vicksburg at the same time, to co-operate with the force moving from Memphis; the purpose being to destroy all the supplies in the rich prairie section of Mississippi and Alabama. The weather was intensely cold, and our men were scantily clad. Great numbers of them suffered severely from frost-bite. General Chalmers notified General Forrest of the situation, and at the same time disposed of the command to meet the advancing Federals. McCulloch was left at Panola, Bell sent to Belmont, Richardson to Wyatt, and McQuirk to Abbeville. The balance of the command was sent to Oxford, where General Chalmers made his headquarters, and at which place General Forrest rejoined us.

While we remained at Oxford, quite a number of the new men whom General Forrest had recruited in West Tennessee decided they could not endure the cold and suffering, and therefore determined to leave the service and return home. This was a serious matter, and required severe and heroic action to check it. As soon as the fact was reported, General Forrest sent men to capture and bring them back. Fifteen or twenty were caught, and carried before General Forrest, who ordered them to be shot the next day. He had coffins made for each, and a long grave dug. The crowd sentenced consisted of ten boys and seven men. Intense excitement prevailed in the neighborhood and among the troops. Delegations of ladies and ministers appealed to General Forrest to spare the men, but he was obdurate. He said he would have no such worthless thrash disgrace his command. The hour arrived, and the deserters riding on their coffins moved to the spot selected for the execution. Two companies guarded the procession. They arrived at the grave, and each man, with his hands tied behind him, sat on the small end of his coffin waiting for the word fire. The occasion was one of the most serious as well as the most solemn ever witnessed by those present. Several hundred soldiers stood around to see what the end would be, and large numbers of citizens and little children were there. The two companies moved to position and loaded their guns. Every thing was in readiness awaiting the command. Who can realize the thoughts that crossed the minds of those men and boys, as they sat on the crumbling brink of eternity, and looked into the interminable abyss? It was awful! People waited for the command "fire." The officer seemed to hesitate, but every one knew it must be done. Those brave, tried and true men, who stood in line with their guns at a ready were suffering almost as much as the deserters. Their faces were pale, but stern. It was the greatest trial of their lives, but they were steady. There was not the slightest quiver. The officer passed in front of the soldiers, and took his position on the right, and faced to the left. The time was short now. Only a moment left for those human beings who had disgraced themselves and the cause. They were doomed.

"Here comes General Forrest," some one said, and he rode hurriedly up in front of the condemned.

He said: "Captain, untie those men and turn them loose," then turning to the deserters said: "Now, boys, you go to your commands, and see if you can't make good soldiers."

General Forrest rode rapidly back to town, and the men who had marched in that solemn procession for execution were free. The town was wild. The terrible gloom which hung over the place gave way to cheers. Men and children went running from house to house telling the news. An hour before both soldiers and citizens were in the depths; now they moved about and laughed. What a wonderful thing is the human mind!

General Forrest was overrun by people expressing appreciation for his pardon of the men. It was a master stroke. There were no more desertions, and the men learned that General Forrest was not cruel, nor unnecessarily severe, but they also learned that he would not be trifled with. The effect was marvelous. The old soldiers who had served under him laughed and said: "We knew he would do it," and the recruits said: "me too."

This circumstance was talked about throughout the South, and hundreds of people heard that the boys were shot.

They censured General Forrest greatly, and there are to-day men and women who believe that the men were killed. They have never forgiven General Forrest. But the writer was with General Forrest nearly two years, and closely associated with his campaigns. The statement, as detailed above, is true in every particular. Forrest seemed to know by instinct what was necessary to do. He was pleasant and companionable when he was not disturbed, but no occasion ever arose which he was not master of. He fought to kill, but he treated his prisoners with all the consideration in his power. So he did his own men. But he wanted the latter for service, and not merely to count. I state it with confidence, that any man who followed Forrest was a good one. He could not stay unless he was. A man who can show that he was with Forrest the last year and a half of the war is no ordinary man, you can depend on that.

On January 11, 1864, the enemy left Memphis, moving east. Sherman began his march to Meridian at the same time. The army leaving Memphis was commanded by General Sooy Smith. General Forrest, after consultation with General Chalmers, telegraphed General Polk he thought it best to concentrate all the available forces against Smith and whip him, after which attention could be given to Sherman. General Polk approved the plan, and promised to send all the troops he could to assist us. It was the evident purpose of the enemy to march on Meridian, and there decide whether to go to Selma or Mobile. It was well known to Sherman that we had but a small force, and this move would necessarily divide it. The Confederate Government received a large proportion of the supplies for the army from the section which the enemy sought to impoverish and desolate. It was, therefore, a most trying situation. Either of the columns, Smith's or Sherman's, greatly outnumbered our forces, and yet these two armies must not come together. How could it be prevented?

On January 14, 1864, General Chalmers reached Houston with his division, while Barteau was marching toward Okalona. The following day the entire command halted at and around Okalona. We found worlds of corn in pens along the line of the Mobile and Ohio Railroad. It was our first trip to the prairies. The horses were fed all they could eat. It was a blessing to them. A cavalry-man thinks first of his horse. It was the first time in weeks that the horses had sufficient feed. General Forrest went to West Point, so as to be in communication with General Polk, and left General Chalmers in command. The enemy was moving on us. General Polk telegraphed General Forrest that he was hurrying a brigade to his support. General Forrest sent word to General Chalmers to hold his ground as long as he could, without bringing on a general conflict. We fell slowly back toward West Point, skirmishing over every foot of the route. General Chalmers was so stubborn in his retreat that several times General Smith made disposition for battle, but as soon as he was ready, we fell back a few miles and went through the same tactics. We reached West Point, and crossed to the south side of the Sookatoncha river, on January 19th. The enemy, in the meantime, was busily engaged burning every thing that could be of any service. At night we could see fires for miles. They burned houses, cribs, fences, and every thing they found.

    On January 20th, the enemy camped near West Point, Mississippi. Early on the morning of the 21st, we crossed the Sookatoncha, with McCulloch's and Jeffrey Forrest's brigades. General Forrest was with us. Those of the enemy who were not engaged burning the houses and property of defenseless citizens were resting quietly in camp. General Forrest, at the head of Jeffrey Forrest's brigade, struck the enemy near West Point. They were not looking for us. Forrest dashed at them in front, and McCulloch's brigade slashed them in the flank. They were surprised, and fled in confusion. We had them flying in twenty minutes. The enemy ran for their lives. We drove them about five miles, when they formed on a line of hills. There was an open field for a full quarter of a mile in their front. As soon as our troops poured out of the woods, the enemy sent a line charging down the hill to meet us. General Smith had his artillery massed on his left flank, from which he rained shot and shell upon our line. McCulloch was in front. It looked as if he could not check that charge, nor stand the fury of the artillery; but "Old Black Bob," with his long saber raised above his head, called on his men to charge. They did not disappoint him. They raised a yell and rushed on. The men acted as if they were inspired. Colonel Forrest and part of his brigade rode rapidly to the left, seeking the enemy's rear, and struck him in the flank about the time McCulloch met him in front. General Forrest rushed forward with McCulloch. It was but a short time before the enemy was in full retreat. We had a running fight nearly to Okalona, and but for night coming on, and the bad condition of the roads and fields, there is no telling what would have been the result. The enemy retreated as fast as we could advance. He used the road, while it was necessary for us to use the fields, in order to get in his rear. Every man was in the saddle by daylight the next morning. General Forrest learned that the enemy had formed a line for battle just in the suburbs of Okalona. He ordered Jeffrey Forrest to attack on the right flank, while McCulloch was sent to the left. Barteau, with his command and the artillery, he posted in front. It was evident that General Smith intended to make the fight of his life right there.

Our troops advanced about the same time from each position. The enemy was well posted. It did not look reasonable that we could drive that long line with the small force we had. But the advance was ordered, and our men went to work. Barteau's line advanced beautifully. Jeffrey Forrest met a strong resistance. So did McCulloch, with whom General Forrest was. Forward they moved. The enemy poured a terrific fire on us, and fought stubbornly. Jeffrey Forrest, at the head of the gallant Seventh Tennessee, was shot, and fell, but the line did not halt. In a few minutes General Forrest was apprised of his death. He galloped to where he lay, and dismounted. He kneeled down and raised Jeffrey's head. He held him in a sitting position a moment, kissed him, and gently placed him back on the ground. He spread his handkerchief over his face, and mounted his horse. Two of his staff, Major J. P. Strange and Captain Charles Anderson, together with his escort, were silent witnesses to that sad scene. They knew how devoted General Forrest was to Jeffrey, and they knew the terrible ordeal he was passing through. But when he mounted he left his heart by Jeffrey's side, and carried madness and destruction in his saddle. He called on "Gaus," his bugler, to sound the charge, and at the head of his escort, with Major Strange and Captain Anderson by his side, he flew to the enemy's flank. In the meantime our men were driving the line back. General Forrest rushed over and rode down the enemy in his front. A panic soon followed. McCulloch had advanced his line nearly a mile, while Barteau drove them from the center. There was now a complete rout. The enemy ran in disorder, throwing away their guns and every thing which impeded their speed. General Forrest continued to repeat: "Charge them! charge them!" He was bent on the destruction of that army. But our troops and horses were completely exhausted. They were compelled to get their breath. He, therefore, withdrew the pursuit.

General Gholson, with about a thousand State troops, reached us early on the morning of the 23d, and hounded the retreating enemy all day. Just as the enemy's lines broke, Colonel McCulloch was painfully wounded. We lost a number of gallant men, among them Lieutenant-Colonel James A. Barksdale, killed at the head of his regiment. He was an ideal man and soldier. No braver man ever gave his life to a patriotic cause. General Smith was so badly whipped that he made no halt until he reached Memphis. He left there with eight thousand or more men, splendidly equipped, cavalry and artillery, with a large train of wagons, confident he would join Sherman. It did not occur to him or his men that Forrest, with his undisciplined force of about thirty-five hundred men, could stay the march an hour. We killed and wounded several hundred of the enemy, and captured many more; together with a large number of wagons and a portion of his artillery and horses. Prior to this fight, even the admirers of Forrest would say that his success was due somewhat to circumstances. But this occasion proved that he was the genius of battle. Think of it just a moment! General Smith, with nearly five thousand men in excess of Forrest's entire force, routed and sent flying back over the road he came. On his march to West Point, his men, after burning every thing in reach, would tell the old men and women who begged for their property what they would do to Forrest and Chalmers when they caught them. These same old people had the satisfaction of seeing the rascals running for their lives, willing to beg pardon or do any thing to keep from meeting Forrest.

    In the meantime Sherman was marching on Meridian, with little or no resistance in his way. When finally he reached that point, and heard of the defeat of Smith, he folded his wings and returned to Vicksburg, without accomplishing any object, except to burn and destroy every thing in his path. Provisions he could not find transportation for he burned. He positively left nothing on his trail for the helpless women and children to eat. The greatest suffering for days and weeks was undergone by those poor people whom he had robbed. Every horse, mule, and cow was driven off. Ladies appealed to him to leave them one horse or cow, and a few rations of meal, but I challenge the world to produce a person who will say that Sherman was ever touched by the pleadings of any woman, even though she asked for what belonged to her. Like the eyeless cobra, he plunged his deadly fangs into every thing that moved within his reach.

CHAPTER SEVENTEEN

How the Boys Sang the Praise of the Starkville Girls – Colonel Young and Lieutenant Taylor Play a Game of Cards – The Battle of Fort Pillow – Conduct of the Negroes – How Forrest Looked

After the fight at Okalona, the entire command was distributed between Starkville and Columbus. The abundance of corn stored in pens and stacks of fodder and hay furnished the opportunity to put the horses in good condition. Company officers were required to look after horses under their charge. The experienced cavalryman took good care of his own horse. He knew the value of having him in good condition, but the men recently enlisted (and they constituted about one-half of the command) thought more of their own comfort than that of their horses. All this had to be looked after, and the men taught the important lesson of true horsemanship. A man who understands how to ride is never troubled with a sore-backed horse. We had an entire regiment of expert horsemen, and we had regiments that had to learn the art, even after the Okalona fight. General Forrest made his headquarters at Columbus, where the people were devotedly attached to him. No Federal command had ever reached Columbus, and the people believed that Forrest would prevent them from ever doing so. General Forrest was fond of company, and spent the time there most pleasantly. The ladies presented him with a magnificent horse, which became almost as famous as the general himself. His name was "King Phillip." He was perfectly white with dark mane and tail. He was a model saddle horse, and made of the same kind of stuff that the general was. We would like to see a monument erected over "Old Phillip." He was buried, after the war, on the general's farm in Coahoma county, Mississippi. Further on we will tell of King Phillip's virtues.

General Chalmers made his headquarters, near Starkville, at the pleasant home of Mrs. Montgomery. It was a comfortable and delightful place. The general and his staff spent a most pleasant ten days halt and rest there. Captain Herbert, formerly on the staff of General Imboden of General Lee's army, had but a short while previous to this reported to General Chalmers for duty, and was temporarily a member of the staff. Major H. H. Chalmers, a younger brother of the general, had been elected a few months before the time we write of, district attorney for North Mississippi. His home, Hernando, was frequently in the enemy's lines, therefore, he did service as a volunteer aid, except when his court was in session. Major Chalmers, or as we familiarly called him, "Major Ham," was an exceedingly bright and talented man. He was subsequently chief justice for Mississippi. We introduce these gentlemen, because they figured quite prominently about that time. Mrs. Montgomery had a very bright, pretty daughter, who also had a troop of attractive young lady friends. A number of these were fine performers on the piano, and several of them were sweet vocalists. Herbert was an accomplished fiddler, and, therefore, was in the "swim from start to finish." After dinner each day, the young ladies, to the number of seven or eight, would come over and listen to Herbert's violin. First one and then the other of them would accompany him on the piano, and frequently all hands would join in a song. We soon discovered that we were delightfully located. The young ladies invariably remained to supper, after which we again repaired to the parlor to enjoy the music and dancing. General Chalmers was the life of the party. His bright speeches and cultured manner gave a freedom to all present. There was no stiffness or formality. The young ladies were gracious and hospitable, and, except when we were on duty in the forenoon, the entire crowd was in the parlors forgetful of war or any other troubles. Major Chalmers also added to the pleasures and amusements of the company. Very naturally the young men of the party were soon "heels over head in love." Each was devoted to the girl of his choice, except that Mills and Lindsay were in love with the same beautiful little widow. Major Chalmers gave all the assistance and encouragement he could to the boys. He would pair them off and watch their progress, but he was taking mental notes all the while. A few evenings before we broke camp, he requested one of the ladies to play for him the accompaniment to "The Hog-eye Man," and he would sing them a song. He surprised us by singing the following:

The Starkville Girls

Air: *Hog Eye-man.*

Of Starkville girls we sing the praise,
How dear they are, how sweet their waves.
Oh! Chalmers' staff will ne'er forget
The day when first these girls they met.

> *Chorus,*
> The pretty little girls of Starkville,
> The pretty little girls of Starkville,
> Oh how they made our hearts to thrill,
> Those pretty little girls of Starkville.

Oh, we'll remember each dear one,
And all the frolic and the fun,
Where we forgot amid their charms
This cruel war and its alarms.

> *Chorus,*
> Those pretty little girls, etc.

Miss Eddins is a stately queen,
By Herbert's side she's ever seen.
There is nobody who can win
Against the man with the violin.

Chorus,
  Those pretty little girls, etc.

Miss Thompson's music can't be beat;
She gave to us a splendid treat.
Her touch is firm, her voice is sweet,
Her equal we will never meet.

Chorus,
  Those pretty little girls, etc.

And then there is Miss Sallie Glenn,
Who plays the wiles with all the men.
Of handsome beaus she has no lack,
From Mississip' to Rackansack.

Chorus,
  Those pretty little girls, etc.

Who can forget Miss Stella fair,
Her grace so sweet and beauty rare.
Oh! his will be a happy life
Who wins this jewel for his wife.

Chorus,
  Those pretty little girls, etc.

What shall we say of Mrs. Nash?
Of all our hearts she made a smash.
Most of us know not what to do,
For two, at least, "went up the flue."

Chorus,
  This pretty little widow of Starkville,
  This pretty little widow of Starkville.
  Oh, how she made our hearts to thrill,
  That pretty little widow of Starkville.

Poor Lindsay died in life's young spring,
And to his grave these flowers we bring,
While tougher Mills with many a gash,
Still lives to sing of Mrs. Nash.

Chorus,
  This pretty little widow, etc.

And now, we've sung of all but one;
Her name is Nannie Middleton.
In beauty's deck she is a trump
She knocked the flinders out of Crump.

>*Chorus,*
>Those pretty little girls, etc.

Of course it was immensely popular, and very soon the whole party sang the major's song. It gave the young ladies more pleasure than all the wooing the boys had done in the past several days. The following evening the young ladies gave notice that they would sing an original song themselves. After supper, quite a crowd, ten or more girls, collected about the piano and sang the following to the tune of "Bobbing Around:"

General Chalmers came to town,
Bobbing around, around, and around.
He and his staff do things up brown,
As they go bobbing around.

Then there is the general's brother,
Bobbing around, around, and around.
But he's not very much like t'other,
As he goes bobbing around.

A brave soldier Capt'n Goodman is.
Bobbing around, around, and around.
A home and pretty wife are his,
While he goes bobbing around.

And then there's Colonel Casey Young.
Bobbing around, around, and around.
His praises are on many a tongue,
As he goes bobbing around.

Now Herbert comes, and Crump, and Mills,
Bobbing around, around, and around.
They've crossed the valleys and the hills,
As they go bobbing around.

O'Neil is good and so is Banks,
Bobbing around, around, and around.

They win the ladies' smiles and thanks,
As they go bobbing around.

There's Lindsay, who no duty shuns,
Bobbing around, around, and around.
And Dinkins, who from ladies runs,
And all go bobbing around.

We know each one will cut a swell,
Bobbing around, around, and around.
But we, alas! must say farewell,
While they'll go bobbing around.

Oh! how we wish that they would stay,
Bobbing around, around, and around.
For they will take our hearts away,
And go on bobbing around.

The following day General Forrest sent a message to General Chalmers requesting his presence at Columbus. Orders were given our servants to have the horses ready at 8 A.M. We gave notice of the intended departure. The young ladies were unusually attractive that night, and we lingered in the parlors until after twelve.

The intention was to say good-bye, but Crump and Lindsay insisted that the ceremony should be postponed until morning. The hour had arrived. It was a memorable scene to us. Our stay had been so pleasant it was with difficulty we tore ourselves away.

Finally the general said: "Young gentlemen, we must be going." We followed him. He was mounted on his little sorrel thoroughbred, The girls waived their handkerchiefs, and said: "Good-bye, good-bye." The general, no doubt, conscious of the delightful entertainment we had enjoyed, allowed the little sorrel too easy a rein. He was the best and fastest saddle animal in the army, and hundreds of men of Chalmers' division will recollect him. The little sorrel felt good. He went skimming over the road in a running walk, that forced the rest of us to gallop, except Colonel Young's colt; he was walking. We reached Columbus for dinner, and found comfortable quarters at the beautiful home of

Colonel Pope, where we met numbers of refined and cultivated people. Most of us endured the separation from Starkville friends without complaint, though Mills and Lindsay spent most of the time in solitude. The little widow had charmed them. They longed to go back for a day, but were ashamed to ask for permission. They were rivals and could not comfort each other. They were miserable, but time and distance cures all such aches. They survived many years, and married other girls.

While at Columbus, our force was augmented by a small brigade of Kentuckians under command of General Abe Buford. The second division of Forrest's cavalry was formed, consisting of two brigades. The first commanded by Colonel A. P. Thompson, and the second by Colonel T. H. Bell. Both brigades mustered twenty-eight hundred effective men. General Buford was given command of the second division. This occurred on March 8, 1864. Soon afterward General Forrest decided to destroy Sherman's communications. He left Columbus with Buford's division and the Seventh Tennessee and McDonald's battalion of Chalmers' division, about the middle of March. He moved directly to Sherman's rear, capturing a number of block houses and garrisons, accomplishing wonderful feats of diplomacy, and destroying over a million dollars worth of supplies. On the 13th of March he ordered General Chalmers to post his division along the Tallahatchie, and protect the country from raids and marauding parties, which were in the habit of going out from Memphis. General Chalmers made his headquarters at Grenada. He established a picket line along the Coldwater river. While the commands were camped on the south bank of the Tallahatchie, Henderson's scouts operated around Memphis in advance of the picket line. Captain Thomas Henderson, who commanded the scouts, was a man of unusual capacity, and, though lame from a wound he had formerly received, was as active on horseback as the best of them. General Chalmers sent Lieutenant Bleecker with a squad of ten men on March 24th to scout in the vicinity of the Memphis and Charleston Railroad. His instructions were to find Captain Henderson and confer with him. Captain Henderson was near Byhalia, and proceeded with Lieutenant Bleecker to Germantown, and they remained two or three days in the neighborhood. While there they heard of Forrest's destruction of the garrisons along Sherman's lines of communication. The men were scouting for news, and Captain Henderson suggested that it would be better for Lieutenant Bleecker and himself to go back to the Byhalia neighborhood, so that the scouts operating in the vicinity of the Mississippi river could reach them quickly. They reached a farm house (the house of Mrs. Williams) at noon, and were invited to stop for dinner. There was a grove around the front of the house, inclosed by a strong rail fence. The "big gate" was some two hundred yards from the house, which was inclosed in a picket fence. The garden to the rear of the house had also a high picket fence around it. The captain and lieutenant hitched their horses on the inside of the yard fence.

They were enjoying a good meal, when Miss Williams, who faced the "big gate," said, "There come the Yankees, run quickly." Lieutenant Bleecker reached the horses in less time than it takes to write it, unhitched both, mounted his own, and led Captain Henderson's to him. About one hundred of the enemy were racing through the grove toward the house. In the meantime Captain Henderson and Bleecker mounted and flew toward the garden. That was the only hope of escape. As they turned the corner of the house they saw Miss Williams holding the gate open. The Yankees were firing their carbines and crying halt. The bullets whizzed about them, and many struck the fence near where Miss Williams stood. Into the garden they rode, Lieutenant Bleecker ahead. There was little hope of the horses clearing the fence, but it was worth a trial. Lieutenant Bleecker rode a large bay, by no means a good jumper, nor was he a fast runner, but the sharp spurs striking his sides made him do his best. The fence was fully six feet high. As he reached it, Bleecker raised himself in the stirrups for the jump. It is known that a horse in jumping gathers his legs under his body and throws them forward just as he alights. Bleecker's horse went at the fence, striking the top railing with his breast, and knocked down the entire panel, falling with it. Captain Henderson was riding a better horse, which cleared Bleecker and his horse as they fell. Both were up, however, in two seconds, and followed Captain Henderson into the woods, making their escape. Captain Henderson when riding carried his crutch on his arm. After reaching a safe distance they halted, and discovered the crutch had the lower end shot off. With this exception neither of them was struck. They remained in the woods until night, and rode back to ascertain what the enemy proposed doing, and found they had returned to Memphis. It was a scouting party, sent out to catch any rebels who might be found in the country.

Lieutenant Bleecker, on the 29th of March, returned to Grenada, with the information that no preparations were being made for an immediate movement. About the 2d of April, Captain Henderson reported that Grierson would leave Memphis in a few days to go in the direction of Baldwin, thence through the prairie country. General Chalmers, in order to prevent Grierson from doing so, moved into West Tennessee with all his force, except four companies left to guard the crossings. Grierson left Memphis, knowing that General Chalmers was north of him, and proceeded toward Okalona. General Forrest was at the same time returning from his raid. Colonel Crews, with McDonald's Battalion, met Grierson, and attacked him with so much vigor that he returned to Memphis. Lieutenant Bleecker did not see the fight made by McDonald's Battalion on that occasion, therefore, can not remember the details sufficiently to do justice to those heroic and invincible men, but it was represented as a brilliant fight, and some one of that band should write it up.

It had been raining heavily for two days before General Chalmers reached Rocky Ford, where he crossed the Tallahatchie, and the river was so swollen that we were delayed several hours before it was low enough to cross. The men lounged about, grazing their horses, telling stories, and whiling away the time in pleasantry and freedom.

Colonel Casey Young was displaying a two dollar greenback, when Lieutenant J. A. Taylor (the late lamented United States district attorney for West Tennessee) remarked that he had a dollar greenback. Colonel Young proposed to play Taylor a game of seven-up for both bills. It was agreed and they straddled a log for the contest. Crowds of men gathered about to watch the game, displaying as much interest as men usually do at a horse race. The crowd was divided; both gentlemen had their backers and partisans. Bets were offered by the Young men, which were taken by the Taylor men, and vice versa. There was nothing to do but pass the time while we waited for the river to fall, therefore the game of seven-up was interesting. The cards were dealt and the money laid on the log. They played several hands and stood, Young six, Taylor three. Another deal by Young; both picked up the cards. Young was bold and aggressive; Taylor carefully scanned his hand, his face a study. The interest was intense. Probably never in their lives before, and maybe never afterward, was it greater. There was a strong probability that Taylor would lose his dollar. Not only the dollar, but his reputation was at stake. He changed the position of his cards repeatedly. The crowd grew larger and larger to watch the game. Men bet all they had on the result. The queen of hearts was turned up. Taylor held jack, ace and three of hearts, ace and four of clubs, and king of spades. A little tow-headed boy who lived in the neighborhood was looking on. He passed to the rear of Taylor and saw his hand, then went over and looked at Young's hand. He knew that Taylor was behind. He no doubt felt a sympathy for him. Young was firing into Taylor and aggravating him in every conceivable way. The boy took a second careful look at Young's hand, and said to Taylor, "Mister, don't you be feared, he aynt got nary one." The words barely passed his lips, when the colonel slapped him entirely over, and fell off the log himself, which saved the boy. I think he would have thrown him in the river had he caught him. But the boy was fleet and realized the value of the gift just at that time. The hand was played. Taylor made high, low, jack, and game. A yell went up from Taylor's crowd as he raked in the greenbacks.

  The tow-headed boy, who had been watching from a safe distance, hallowed out, "I'm glad un it; I'm glad un it." Every thing was lost to Colonel Young, except the colt and Uncle Bedney. His reputation was gone. He felt he was ruined. He had practiced seven-up by the dim light of the camp-fire, had made a reputation, and had nursed it tenderly, but, like all things earthly, it was swept away. These reflections no doubt passed through his mind as he walked over where Uncle Bedney stood grazing the colt. The tow-headed boy recognized him, and said again, "I'm durned glad un it." But he was sorry that minute he said it. He smelled sulphur and brimstone. Great volumes rolled out of the colonel's mouth. Taylor was the hero of the hour. His crowd followed him about, offering to back him with all they had.

We soon crossed the river and moved toward Jackson, where in a few days we met General Forrest, with the Seventh Tennessee and McDonald's Battalion. He reached us in advance of Buford's division. We spent several days very pleasantly at Jackson. General Forrest was told by citizens living in the direction of Fort Pillow, that bands of Federal and Negro soldiers made frequent raids through the country, robbing people of any thing they could find, and insulting in the grossest possible manner any lady who protested against their action. The Negro soldiers were especially insulting to the wives and families of Confederate soldiers. In some cases, they committed an unpardonable, brutish, and fiendish crime on ladies. Numbers of our men lived in that country, and they joined in the appeal to General Forrest to give them protection. He decided to do so, and early on the morning of April 11, 1864, General Chalmers, with McCulloch's and Bell's brigades and Walton's battery, marched out to clear the country of the rascals. Before day on the morning of April 12th, we halted in front of Fort Pillow. It had been raining all night, and was so dark it was difficult to keep the road, or even see the men beside you. The advance guard was accompanied by an old gentleman who lived near Fort Pillow. He was thoroughly acquainted with the ground. The advance guard passed around to the rear of the Federal pickets, who were captured without firing a gun, and as soon as this was accomplished, General Chalmers pressed rapidly forward with McCulloch's brigade and took possession of the outer works. These ditches were built by our own people, before Fort Pillow fell into the hands of the Federals. Inside of them, other and better works had been thrown up. General Chalmers directed McCulloch to extend his lines toward the river, and Bell was sent on the north side, with instructions to open the fight, which would engage the attention of the enemy and enable McCulloch to advance and secure a position under the enemy's guns. Bell could not, however, make the attack as soon as was expected, on account of the very rough ground, so General Chalmers ordered "Colonel Black Bob" to advance. He did so, and secured the protection of a lot of cabins just outside the fort. Just at that time General Forrest reached us. He conferred with General Chalmers, who advised him of the situation. The enemy felt perfectly secure, and had no idea that any force could successfully storm their position. They waved their hats, telling our men: "Come on, you dirty rebels." The Negro soldiers were particularly offensive in offering banters.

General Forrest saw the invitations and banters, and determined to accommodate the scoundrels. He ordered the line to advance, and our men pushed forward across the gullies and over the rough ground, under a heavy fire from the fort. The Negro soldiers had been given all the whisky they could drink, and were told that no rebel troops could ever enter Fort Pillow. They exposed themselves above the works, firing at our line, and cursing and daring us to come on. We reached the ditch just under the big fort, which was below the big guns, and so near them that they could not be depressed sufficiently to damage us. While in this position, General Forrest said to General Chalmers: "We better give them a chance to surrender." General Chalmers then said to Captain W. A. Goodman, his adjutant-general: "Tie your handkerchief on a stick, and we will put you over the wall. Tell Major Booth, General Forrest desires to avoid any sacrifice of life, and therefore will give him an opportunity to surrender. If he refuses, say to him, the men are in no humor to be brought face to face with the Negro soldiers who have insulted their families." Captain Goodman found that Major Booth had been killed, and that a Major W.F. Bradford, of the Thirteenth Tennessee Battalion, was in command. Bradford delayed his answer fully an hour, believing, no doubt, that the firing had attracted the attention of some of the Federal gun-boats, and that they would come to his assistance. General Forrest knew his game, and at the expiration of an hour, said: "Tell him I will give him twenty minutes, and that is all I will give. If he does not surrender, I will not be responsible for the conduct of my men. Tell him this plainly." While we waited for the end of the twenty minutes, and it seemed about two hours, we could see the smoke from several boats coming up the river. As the front boat turned the bend, we saw she was loaded with troops. There was also a gun-boat anchored out in the river. She was the *New Era*. She did not move, but the steamboat passed by the fort, loaded with infantry and a battery of artillery. The Negroes in the fort looked down at us, and snarled and cursed the rebels. Finally, Captain Goodman, at the end of the time granted, returned to say they would not surrender. General Forrest, up to this time, did not seem to be much concerned or in any wise disturbed, but he changed in a second. He said: "General Chalmers, tell your men to plant their flags on that cursed fort, and take what they find." He moved along the line in the ditch, talking to the men, saying: "At 'em! at 'em!" He was the incarnation of all the destructive powers on earth. He was to a battle what a cyclone is to an April shower. His voice could be heard by the Yankees. No doubt they trembled, as later events proved.

The guns on the fort looked savage. General Chalmers told McCulloch to designate one regiment to open on the fort and keep the enemy back, while the balance went over the bank. General Forrest called out: "Blow the charge, Gaus, blow the charge." The impetuosity of the attack was remarkable. The men had stood by and heard and saw what was going on. Their families and friends had been insulted and outraged. They were ready and eager to avenge those wrongs, and, before the enemy had any thought on the subject, those ragged rebels were climbing and pushing each other over the wall. The outside of the fort was in ridges, caused by heavy rains washing out gullies. These afforded hand holds to the men in climbing up. As soon as our men began to mount the top of the fort, the garrison took to their heels. They wanted to reach the water's edge, so they could secure the protection of the gun-boat. They had been told that the rebels could not get over the works and into the fort, and did not believe they could, but the sight of the "Johnnies" was a flat contradiction of the blustering lie. They ran with all their speed. Our men the blustering lie. They ran with all their speed. Our men called on them to halt, firing at them as they ran. Not one, however, would halt, unless a bullet caught him. They ran to the high bluff and jumped over. Those who did never knew what the end was. They were too flat to bury. The gun-boat made no effort to help them, neither did the steamboat, with the troops on board, make a landing. Why, we could never imagine. They could have made it awfully hot for us. The Negroes went over the bluff like sheep going through a gate. They would jump as high as they could. They would not surrender. Both Generals Forrest and Chalmers, seeing the panic, called on the men to cease firing, and after a few minutes succeeded in restoring order. From the time Captain Goodman reported, until the fight was over, it was not exceeding ten minutes. Numbers of the garrison were drowned. Those who reached the river never stopped, but plunged in. They were frightened out of all reason. After the fight, General Forrest requested the officers of the gun-boat to come ashore and bury their dead, and take the wounded; but no, sir, they would not land among that crowd. We had not over eighteen hundred men, while the enemy had about seven hundred men in the seemingly impregnable fort. Our loss was nearly one hundred killed and wounded.

After the capture, General Forrest returned to Jackson, saying to General Chalmers: "See that the dead are buried, and the wounded cared for, then burn every thing." The Yankee soldiers and Negroes, both dead and wounded, were lying as they had fallen. General Chalmers had those of the prisoners who were not wounded, and also some of our own men at work burying the dead. Some of the Negroes, smarter than the others, were lying flat on their faces, pretending to be dead. When one of them was reached, the men began to dig his grave near where he lay. He raised his head just a little, and said: "Marster, for God's sake, spare me; I didn't want to leave home; dey 'scripted me. Spare me, marster, and take me home. Dey 'scripted me." He was spared, and many others in the same way. In fact, not one of the garrison, white or black, was mistreated. But I believe that any other people, under similar circumstances, would have killed every

Negro in the fort. The feeling which a Southern man has for a Negro is difficult for others to understand. He was regarded then as a piece of property, and when he did wrong was treated in the same way that a refractory horse or child would be. He must be brought into subjection, after which there was no feeling of bitterness. Our men felt outraged, and killed every rascal as long as they resisted or ran. But, when they had been captured, they were as safe as they could have been anywhere.

After the destruction of Fort Pillow, we moved via Jackson to Okalona. The command had been actively engaged for some time, and the beautiful prairies of East Mississippi, with plenty of corn and fodder, were just what the men and horses needed.

"On, Girls! The one in the middle has got on a corset."

CHAPTER EIGHTEEN
A Season of Rest in the Rich Mississippi Prairies –
The Battle of Brice's Cross Roads – A Jackson Girl
Accuses Bleecker of Wearing a Corset –
A Tournament at Egypt – General Sturges
Promises to Capture Forrest –
The Death of Billy Pope

☆ ☆ ☆ ☆

The news that Fort Pillow had been destroyed gave happiness to thousands of people. It had been a place where the worst class of Negroes and other disreputable characters congregated. On the march toward Okalona, the people along the road cheered the men and praised them for the work they had done. General Chalmers, with his staff and escort, rode ahead to Jackson, remaining there a day and night, and stopping at the hotel. The young men of the staff, Bleecker, Taylor, and Lindsay, while strolling through the town, passed a place where there were several pretty girls standing at the gate. Bleecker always wore his coat closely buttoned. He was walking between Lindsay and Taylor. After they passed, one of the girls remarked: "Oh, girls, that one in the middle has got on a corset." Then they all laughed heartily. Bleecker never had his manhood so criticised and shocked before. He knew he was short in many respects. He knew he had committed sundry errors, but to be accused, or even suspected, of wearing a corset, was a little more than he was prepared to stand. Taylor and Lindsay rasped him, and told the general, and other members of the staff, what the girls had said. Bleecker had warm friends in the escort company. They guyed him. He felt that life had become a burden. He prided himself on his horsemanship. He was an expert with a six-shooter. He had seen three years' service in the army, but to have it said he wore a corset, knocked all the egotism, pride, and confidence out of him.

On reaching Okalona, we went into camp. The citizens were glad to welcome Forrest's cavalry back. There was plenty of forage for the horses, and plenty of bread and meat for the men. General Chalmers made his headquarters at the home of Colonel W.G. Henderson. Colonel Henderson formerly belonged to the Army of Northern Virginia, but was now the colonel of the Fifth Mississippi. Mrs. Henderson was an intelligent, accomplished and attractive woman, and, withal, a good housekeeper. She gave us the best table fare we had known for many a day, and there was plenty of it, too. Colonel Henderson, himself a soldier, knew what a good appetite required, and Mrs. Henderson doubtless measured ours by his. We spent a delightful two weeks there, after which General Chalmers moved near Egypt Station on the Mobile and Ohio Railroad, where forage was abundant. He made his headquarters at the hospitable home of Colonel English. There we had ham, and lamb, and strawberry jam. Mrs. English had a good garden, plenty of rich milk and butter, and all the accessories to make us happy. The weather was warm and beautiful. Living near Colonel English was an elegant family, the McQuistons. There were two young ladies in the family, and Mrs. English also had a little miss not yet grown. Through the kindness of Miss Maggie English, all hands made the acquaintance of Miss McQuiston and Miss Fanny, her sister, who added greatly to the pleasures of the party.

While the command rested in that charming neighborhood, some of the men in the Second Missouri, joined by several of Willis' Texas Battalion, concluded to have a tournament, but of a different kind from the ordinary sort. The ground was selected near a grove in front of which there was a pretty stretch of road, where the riders could be seen in the afternoon practicing for the occasion. There were no posts with projections holding the rings, and there were no lances to be used, but the rings, covered with red cloth, were placed on the ground fifty feet apart.

The distance to be ridden was one hundred yards, to be made in ten seconds, and the rings picked up with the hand. Fully twenty-five gallant fellows spent the afternoon trying to catch the rings as they flew by on their horses. The event attracted much attention, and there were a number of ladies from Aberdeen, seven miles distant, to witness the display of horsemanship. The soldiers made seats for the spectators in the shade of the trees, and built a platform on which the "Queen of Love and Beauty" should be crowned.

When the day arrived, the contestants, reduced to sixteen, were on hand. Colonel A. H. Chalmers, Lieutenant-Colonel Robert A. McCulloch, and adjutant Wm. S. Pope, of the Seventh Tennessee, were selected as judges. The knights were arranged in order and Colonel Willis, the Grand Marshal, announced the rules and called for the first knight. Each one was entitled to three tilts. The knight handing to the judge the greatest number of rings, should select and crown the "Queen of Love and Beauty." It was a rare sight to witness the recklessness of these men and boys. They dashed over the space as fast as their horses could take them, hanging suspended by the left foot, which rested behind the cantel of the saddle, dragging the right hand on the ground. Each knight was cheered, which inspired the next rider to try some new feature. It was great fun. The ladies never saw any thing like it before.

After the tilting, the judges announced that Lieutenant Bleecker captured six rings, which was one more than the number returned by any other knight, and he would, therefore, crown the queen. The announcement elicited hearty cheers from the crowd, both soldiers and citizens, because Bleecker was the youngest among the contestants. After the announcement by the judges, the marshal, followed by all the knights, rode in column before the platform, and halted, facing the audience. Colonel Willis called Bleecker to the front, but he did not move. He said: "Colonel Willis, let some one else go." But Colonel Willis forced him up to the stand, and told him to choose his queen, at the same time handing him a wreath of flowers.

Bleecker sat on his little sorrel, frightened nearly to death.

He whispered to Colonel Willis, hoping no one would hear the name. The colonel called in a loud voice: "Will Miss Fannie McQuiston please come to the stand." Miss Fannie had no idea of going, but her friends finally made her do so. Bleecker had known Miss Fannie only a short time, but he had a high regard for her. She was being escorted to the stand by Colonel Chalmers; Bleecker waited until they were within ten feet of the stand, when he threw the crown to her, and put spurs to his horse. He was out of sight before any one knew what he was about. But that was not the end of the performance. General Chalmers scolded him roundly, and declared he would never introduce him to another girl. Bleecker was more to be pitied than censured, however, for he did not have sufficient nerve. He could face armed foes in battle, but he could not face a bevy of smiling and beautiful girls.

Toward the latter part of May, 1864, General Chalmers was ordered to move to Monte Vallo, Alabama, to defend the iron works, on the North and South Alabama Railroad, against a raid supposed to be contemplated for their destruction. We remained in that section for a few days, and about the 10th of June, received orders to move back to Columbus with all possible dispatch. Every thing was gotten ready, and we began the march the following morning. General Sturgis, in the meantime, with a finely-equipped army of nine thousand cavalry and infantry, twenty-five pieces of artillery, and several hundred wagons, left Memphis to clean up Forrest, and destroy our bread supply, a feat which several Federal generals had started out to accomplish, but none had succeeded in performing. General Sturgis stated to a lady, at whose house near Salem he remained all night on his down trip, that he was after Forrest this time, and if he would stand up and give a chance, and not run away, he would destroy his command and bring Forrest back a prisoner.

The lady replied: "Look out, he may send you back running."

But the general laughed, and said: "No danger, and do not be surprised if I stop on my return with Forrest a prisoner." The proud and confident general moved his army forward in military order, with every thing in proper trim. There was not a suspicion of doubt on his mind. He knew he had three times as many men as Forrest, and he also had a splendid artillery battalion. He therefore went forth full of confidence. It will be remembered that General Chalmers, with McCulloch's brigade, was away in Alabama, so that Forrest only had Buford's division and Rucker's brigade, some three thousand all told, to meet that picked army, and its haughty and boastful commander. The forces met at what is called Brice's Cross Roads, where the Ripley and Guntown roads intersect, four miles west of Baldwin, a station on the Mobile and Ohio Railroad. In General Sturgis' command were two regiments of Negroes, who had taken an oath on their knees before leaving Memphis, in the presence of General Hurlbut, that they would avenge Fort Pillow. That they would take no prisoners. They wore badges on their breasts, "Remember Fort Pillow. Death to Forrest and his men." Our men were not aware of this, however, until during the fight, they saw running Negroes tearing their badges off as they ran.

General Forrest struck Sturgis unawares. He rushed at his column and whipped him before he could gather his forces. Our old ragged boys were feeling good that summer morning. If the story of each individual could be told, the acts of bravery and daring would fill a book. Better soldiers never faced an enemy than those who met Sturgis at Brice's Cross Roads. There was no hesitation, but when the order was given to charge, each man went to work as if the result depended on his individual efforts. They charged in front and on the flank. The advance guard of Sturgis was thrown back in great confusion on his main column. His cavalry rampled down his infantry, followed by the invincible band, of Forrest, which rode them to death or capture. Wagons were capsized, the horses cut loose and used to escape on. The artillery was tumbled against trees or left in the road. There was never such a panic and such a rout before. Most of the cavalry escaped, but the infantry were either killed, wounded, or captured. The Negroes, such as were not killed, took to the woods and ran for their lives. They tore their badges off and threw them away. The oath they took before leaving Memphis must have been taken with a reservation. Our loss was serious, about one hundred and thirty killed and some five hundred wounded. We lost some grand and glorious men, whose names should be written on the lintels of the eternal city. The enemy's loss was terrible. One thousand nine hundred and seventy killed, besides the loss of over two thousand prisoners, including the wounded, fully one thousand more than Forrest's entire force. We also captured twenty pieces of artillery, twenty-one caissons, and two hundred and thirty wagons, besides all his ambulances.

There was a gallant boy who yielded up his life on that day who deserves a page in history. He was bright and handsome, brave and generous, loved by his comrades, and worshiped by a devoted mother and sister. He carried happiness into every circle he entered, and won the confidence of all he met. He was as pure as the rose-bud glistening with the dews of the morning. He gave his life for a cause which did not succeed, but his name will be remembered, and his memory will be cherished. He was killed in the discharge of duty while he rode at the head of his regiment. This hero was "Billy Pope," adjutant of the Seventh Tennessee. Billy and the writer were warm friends. We often talked of home and mothers. Farewell, Billy, may we "meet beyond the river, where the surges cease to roll."

The pursuit was kept up as long as human endurance permitted. The news of the defeat reached Salem before General Sturgis did, and the lady was standing at the gate to see if he had General Forrest. When he left her his uniform was bright and new, but when he returned he was covered with mud. His horse was exhausted, and both presented the appearance of defeat and disaster.

The lady asked: "General, did you find General Forrest?"
"No," General Sturgis replied, "but he found me!"
The battle of Brice's Cross Roads was one of the most brilliant feats in the annals of war. There will probably never again occur such a victory. The future may develop great generals, but none will approach Forrest as a brave, dashing soldier. In the humble opinion of the writer, he was the greatest military man who ever lived, and the future will hardly see his like. The South

will enjoy the distinction of having developed two remarkable characters. The first was Forrest, the only commander of an army in the world's history who never suffered defeat. The second was General Joseph E. Johnson, the only commander of an army known in history who never won a victory.

Chalmers' division remained at Columbus until the first of July, then moved to Tupelo. Buford's division was at Pontotoc. General A.J. Smith, sorely hurt by the defeat of General Sturgis. decided to break up that nest of hornets down in Mississippi. He left Memphis, about July the 3d, with an army of fifteen thousand men. General S.D. Lee at this time assumed personal command of all the troops in Alabama and North Mississippi, his forces numbering some eight thousand men, including about nine hundred infantry brought from Mobile. Chalmers' division was at the point where the Houston and Pontotoc roads cross, the enemy marching southward.

Capt. George Dashiell
of General Forrest's Staff

CHAPTER NINETEEN
General A. J. Smith Captures and Burns Oxford –
Gallant Defense Made By General Chalmers –
The Enemy Burn the Home of Jacob Thompson

On July 7, 1864, General A. J. Smith, with his army, reached Ripley, Mississippi. He was met by our pickets, who skirmished with his advance until he reached New Albany. Smith's forces burned or destroyed every thing in their path. Lone chimneys and piles of ashes, covering a scope ten miles wide, marked the desolation he made. McCulloch was sent to Pontotoc on July the 10th, and was soon afterward joined by General Chalmers, with Rucker's brigade. General Chalmers was instructed to detain the advance of the enemy as long as possible. Buford, in the meantime, with his division, was engaged in watching Smith's left flank. We had fallen back about four or five miles south of Pontotoc, where we camped on the night of July 12th. The following morning, General S. D. Lee, accompanied by General For-rest, reached our position. General Lee decided to give battle. We learned that the enemy was moving toward the east. General Forrest, with his escort and a small force, went in pursuit, hoping to hold him until our command could get up. We moved under General Lee through the woods, expecting to strike Smith on the flank, but he moved faster than we could, and reached Tupelo without much hinderance. On the morning of July 14, 1864, he occupied a range of hills at Harrisburg, where he had advantage in position of any force that might oppose him. He had built breast-works during the night, by stringing a lot of logs around his camp, and these he covered with dirt. However, General Lee determined to attack him, and told General Forrest to prepare for battle. Buford sent his skirmish line forward and opened the fight. Chalmers' division was held as a second line. There was some delay in Roddy's going to the attack, therefore Buford struck the enemy's center, and was driven back. Then Bell and Mabry moved forward, but were also driven back. General Chalmers moved Rucker's brigade to support Mabry, and sent McCulloch to support Buford. Those gallant fellows charged to within fifty yards of the enemy's works, but were driven back. McCulloch and Rucker, both fine brigade commanders, distinguished themselves on that hot July day. Rucker was twice seriously wounded before leaving the field. General Chalmers, by his bravery and daring, saved his division from panic. Fully one-third of both brigades were killed or wounded.

It was apparent to all the men that we could not drive General Smith from his position. His force was nearly double ours, while he was strongly entrenched on a naturally strong position. Soon after noon, General Lee ordered the whole command to fall back, and we remained in line until about night, when the Federals burned the little town of Harrisburg. General Chalmers, with McCulloch's brigade, was ordered to again advance, but was driven back, and both armies spent the night in about the same position they occupied in the morning. Next day, General Lee moved the whole force near to Tupelo, intending to make fight, in case the enemy came out of his strong position. We waited anxiously, and about ten o'clock the scouts reported the enemy was in full retreat. General Lee ordered General Chalmers to press them, which he did. General Buford also moved forward, and rode into an ambuscade in the woods. Bell's brigade was badly cut up, but at this time General Forrest arrived with McCulloch's brigade, which he dismounted and charged through the woods, driving the enemy back. General Chalmers noticed an effort to flank Bell's position, when, with Kelly's regiment, he moved rapidly to the left, and checked the movement; and, notwithstanding these men had been fighting for two days, they responded to General Chalmers' call, and rushed at the enemy with the fierceness of tigers.

What a magnificent body of men those Tennessee boys were. General Forrest was wounded in the charge, as was also Colonel McCulloch, and both were compelled to quit the field, leaving the command to General Chalmers. General Lee, in the meantime, remained at Tupelo, but when General Forrest reached him and reported the situation he joined General Chalmers. Night coming on, the pursuit was withdrawn. The morning of July 16th found our command in the worst condition it had ever known, but General Lee ordered General Chalmers to follow with Rucker's and Roddy's brigades, which he did as well as he could, considering the condition of the horses and men. General Smith retreated, but he left our command in no condition to follow him. The fight at Harrisburg was a great mistake. Forrest's cavalry had never been called on before to do an impossible thing, and the men felt that they had been badly handled. We were whipped on the 14th at Harrisburg, and again the following day near Town Creek. Forrest had always sought the weak point of the enemy, at which he could throw his whole power and create a stampede. Once on the run he pressed his advantage until he converted the stampede into a rout. His men were accustomed to his tactics, and when they were ordered to charge that fortified crest of hills, they moved forward confident of success. They knew our force was nothing like so large as the enemy's, but they were accustomed to disparity in numbers. They had several times routed three to one, and on this occasion there were only two to one against them. They did not doubt their ability, and even when nearly a third of their number had been killed or wounded they stood before those breast-works battering away at the enemy until ordered to withdraw. We lost about fifteen hundred true and brave men. When General Buford withdrew his command and all the firing had ceased, he rode away from the scene and stood alone under the shade of a large tree. General Forrest passing by asked where his command was. General Buford covered his face with his arm, and said: "I have no command. They were all killed." He was deeply grieved, and in no condition to discuss the events of the battle at Harrisburg.

    Colonel McCulloch, after the fight on the 14th of July, superintended in person the care of his wounded. A man of large frame and strong face, who had met the enemy on probably a hundred fields, and was conspicuously known for his bravery and intrepidity, was then administering to his suffering comrades. His strong character had for the moment lost its force. The tension had yielded, and he was a child. His heart was larger than his body. He could not control his feelings. When he found those men who had left their homes in far away Missouri to follow his standard, men who had never failed to move forward when he led, when he found those men dead or wounded, he knelt over them and cried as if his heart would break. He said: "It was cruel. My poor boys were shot down like dogs."

    McCulloch was painfully wounded on the following day. Had the entire force been sent against the enemy at the same moment, the result might have been different, but we fought in detail. Buford was whipped, then Mabry, then McCulloch, then Rucker, and so on. General Lee returned to Meridian on the 17th. The command then devolved on General Chalmers. He sent his division to camp at Oakland Church, about eight miles from Egypt; Buford to Egypt, Roddy to North Alabama, and the infantry was ordered back to Meridian. General Chalmers made his headquarters at Okalona. General Forrest was also at Okalona, at the house of Major Shepherd, suffering very much from the wound in his foot. The command remained in camp until August 1st. In the meantime, General Chalmers ascertained that the enemy was organizing another expedition to leave Memphis, Vicksburg, and North Alabama simultaneously. He conferred with General Forrest, who suggested that he apprise General Lee of the fact, and he wrote General Lee advising that all the forces be concentrated on the column moving from Memphis. On August 1st, the enemy had a force of fifteen thousand infantry and twenty-five pieces of artillery at La Grange, Tennessee. General Chalmers sent McCulloch's brigade to Oxford, on August 2d. Two days later, General Forrest still suffering from his wounds, assumed command, and ordered General Chalmers to follow Mc-

Culloch's brigade and prevent the enemy from crossing the Tallahatchie if possible.

We reached Waterford on the 8th, and began to guard a river front of ten miles, against an army of ten times our numbers. McCulloch and Rucker had both been wounded, as had been several field officers, and officers of the line. On August 8th, General A.J. Smith confronted us at Abbeyville with twenty thousand men. General Forrest, with the balance of the command, was moving with all possible dispatch toward Oxford. The enemy had repaired the Mississippi Central Railroad as far south as the Tallahatchie, and began crossing the river at that point. He shelled the whole country for a mile on the south of the river, and drove our few troops back into the woods. The Eighteenth Mississippi, Colonel A. H. Chalmers, was the only force opposing General Smith. Colonel Chalmers fell back to Hurricane creek, and constructed some rail breastworks. The balance of McCulloch's brigade went to his support. Before General Chalmers reached Hurricane creek, the Eighteenth Mississippi was hotly engaged skirmishing with the enemy. Colonel Chalmers, with great determination, held his position against an overwhelming force.

The following day the enemy moved his force forward, and used his big guns with dreadful effect on the timber. We fell back to Oxford, sternly contesting every foot of the ground. Before we reached Oxford, General Smith concluded to crush our little command, and pressed forward with considerable animation, and as soon as he came within range, began to throw his big shells into the town. General Chalmers moved south, thinking General Hatch would follow with his cavalry, but the latter did not go farther than Oxford. The same night, the enemy returned to Hurricane creek, and soon afterward, General Forrest, with Bell and Mabry's brigades, and Morton's battery, entered Oxford, where General Chalmers joined him the next morning. We advanced our line again to Hurricane creek, when the enemy made a vicious attack on us. Mabry's brigade was about to be overrun, and, but for the dash and courage of the Eighteenth Mississippi (such as was seldom surpassed by any troops), we would have lost our position. General Forrest knew it would not do to bring on an engagement, and, therefore, decided to resort to different tactics. He discussed with General Chalmers what was best to be done, and decided to take part of the command and attack Memphis, while General Chalmers would draw the enemy as far south as he could. The home of the Hon. Jacob Thompson was just in the southern suburbs of the town. Here General Hatch made his headquarters, when he followed us on the 9th. He entered the house uninvited, and went through it as if he had been the master. His coarse, uncultivated, and ungentlemanly manners, satisfied Mrs. Thompson that she could expect no protection from his vandals. His men plundered every thing on the premises, and ruthlessly destroyed the carriage and other property. General Hatch sat in a large upholstered rocking chair in the handsomely furnished hall with big muddy boots on. Mrs. Thompson appealed to him to restrain his men. He answered with coarse and brutal language: "Let them go. They can take any thing they find, and do any thing they want, except take the chair I am sitting in." Soon afterward, he thought it would be safer to have the protection of General Smith's infantry. He had his ambulance filled with pictures, silver plate, china, and such other article as he wanted, many of them of great value, and all of which he carried with him.

Late in the afternoon of August 18, 1864, General Forrest, with some fifteen hundred men and two pieces of artillery, left Oxford for Memphis. General Chalmers remained at Oxford, and on the morning of the 19th, advanced all the picket lines, and made attacks on the enemy at every point. We were hotly engaged until the afternoon, when General Smith advanced his lines again. We fell back to a point about a mile north of Oxford, where we were reinforced by General Buford with his Kentucky brigade. It had been raining for several days, and the swollen condition of the creeks operated somewhat in our favor. Early on the 20th of August, General Chalmers again advanced his lines, and made a vicious rush at the Federals, driving them back to Hurricane creek. But the incessant rains raised the streams so high behind us, it was dangerous to remain so near the large force without the chance of falling back if it became necessary, so that on the 21st he again drove the enemy's picket line in, while he moved the wagons and got the command under headway toward the south. In the meantime, Hatch, with a brigade of cavalry, was moving around, hoping to get in our rear. We fell back to Springdale, leaving the Seventh Tennessee at Oxford to watch and report the movement of the enemy. The Yankees entered Oxford the next morning, and burned the depot, court-house, and all empty buildings and houses. The individual men scattered over the town, setting fire to every place they passed. Nearly every business house in the town was burned, as well as some handsome residences. The beautiful home of Jacob Thompson was the special work for General A. J. Smith. He dignified the occasion by sending a detachment in charge of one of his staff officers to burn it, and he did his work nobly. Mrs. Thompson was in ill-health, with her children to look after. She begged them to spare her home. Before the torch was applied, the Yankee soldiers rifled the house of every thing they wanted, and even a few relics which Mrs. Thompson carried out were taken from her. In the town, carpets were torn up, rugs, silver-ware, and every article of value were stolen. In the morning on which the Yankees entered Oxford, a number of our men loitered about the town. There was a party sitting upstairs over Avant's bank, discussing things in general. Their horses were hitched around at different posts and rings. It was remarkable what chances men would take. They knew there were none of our troops between them and the enemy, and yet they loitered there in the shade, chatting away as cheerfully and as regardless of danger as field-larks. Captain A.D. Bright had his horse hitched to a ring on the sidewalk. His halter rein was a good long one, and the sidewalk was about a foot higher than the street. "Bud Dillard," McCulloch's bugler, a boy about fifteen, was standing on the corner and saw the Yankee cavalry coming down the street. He hardly had time to escape, but he thought of those upstairs. He ran up the steps, shouting: "The Yankees are in town." Down the boys tumbled. They rolled down and on to the sidewalk, and rushed for their horses. Bright forgot his halter rein was fastened to the ring, and mounted his horse and plunged his spurs into him. He bounded off with all his might, and fell broadside on the ground. The halter was broken. Both Bright and the horse rose together, and struck the street flying. The Yankees saw him, and rode for him, firing as they went, calling on him to halt; but Bright had business further south at that time, and having a better horse than his pursuers, made his escape. We never saw Bright until next day, and he told so many tales about where he went, we never knew positively what he did. It was remarkable how the crowd escaped. There were Captain F. Hargraves, Lieutenant Wm. Joyce, Lieutenant Chas. Martin, Colonel Casey Young, and Bright in the party.

CHAPTER TWENTY

General Forrest Makes a Dash Into Memphis – The Effort to Capture Generals Washburn and Hurlbut – Men Ride Into the Gayoso Hotel on Their Horses – The Plight of Federal Prisoners – How General Forrest Fed Them and His Own Men – People Thought Judgment Day Was Coming – The Negro Soldiers' Idea of Forrest

The enemy under General Smith, ignorant of General Forrest's movement, advanced his entire force to Oxford, and after burning the town and resorting to the most cruel and inhuman acts toward the defenseless citizens, was preparing to move further south and destroy that section. About an hour before night, however, they hurriedly began a retreat toward Holly Springs, marching all night. General Chalmers was quickly advised of this, and knew Smith had received information of Forrest's movement, and, notwithstanding muddy roads, moved forward with great rapidity, sending Buford ahead with McCulloch's and the Kentucky brigade, while he in person led Mabry's brigade. Colonel Bill Wade was in command of McCulloch's brigade. He was an old infantry colonel, and had seen service in the Mexican War. Colonel Wade in advance struck the enemy's rear guard, just in the northern suburbs of Oxford. He rode at the head of the Fifth Mississippi, and when he reached the enemy, he formed the men in columns of eight, and with his saber cutting right and left, dashed through the Federal columns. His men used their guns as clubs, and rode over and trampled down a whole regiment. It was a desperate charge, but the men of the Fifth Mississippi were accustomed to desperate work. Wade afterward said: "D—n them. They have been running us for two or three days. I want them to know we are not afraid of them."

The enemy halted after arriving at Hurricane creek, and formed his line, expecting an at-tack. They were evidently getting nervous, and would have retreated in greater haste but for the delay in crossing the Tallahatchie river. We have said very little about the artillery, though much credit is due that branch of the service, for several of Forrest's successes. During the retreat of the enemy on the 23d, Captain Ed. S. Walton, with his battery, performed some wonderful feats. He kept his guns fully up to the front during the whole day, and poured grape and shell into their ranks, crushing and tearing them to pieces. The conduct of Walton and his men was grand. Whenever the enemy fell back, they took right hold of the guns and ran for better position. It was difficult for the cavalry to keep up with them. The constant engagements for several days had exhausted our ammunition, and the horses were worn out, and they had very little feed for two days. Further, General Smith destroyed the bridge over the Tallahatchie, which made it impossible for General Chalmers to pursue the enemy beyond the river.

We returned to Oxford, and found the people in a desperate condition. They had no food of any kind. General Chalmers sent word to hurry all the supplies to Oxford that could be found. Ladies and children were, in many cases, homeless and hungry. Those who were fortunate enough to have their houses left, had nothing to eat, and had to live on soldier's rough meat and bread for several days, and were glad to get that. When the enemy heard that Forrest was in Memphis, they feared he would get in their rear. Numbers of them knew what it was to have him on their trail, and, therefore, sought all the news obtainable. A Captain Cannon seemed very anxious to learn something about Forrest, and inquired of Mr. Cook, a citizen of Oxford, what kind of a man he was. Mr. Cook gave him a description of the general, and asked the Yankee captain if he would be willing to pick one hundred men and meet Forrest with the same number. "No," he replied, "I do not care to fight Forrest alone, with my whole company. I hope I may never see him."

It is remembered that when General Forrest left Oxford, Memphis bound, it had been raining very hard, and continued two days afterward. The creeks were all greatly swollen, and the Tallahatchie river also. The roads were as muddy as rain could make them. It looked like an unwise and a forlorn effort, but with that indomitable and indefatigable man, in the lead of such soldiers as followed him on that expedition, obstacles which other men could not have surmounted, gave way. It was necessary to go as far west as Panola, in order to cross the Tallahatchie. They rode all night in darkness and mud, swimming creeks, and often getting down in the mud and water to pull the artillery over, but they never complained.

They reached Panola about sunrise the next morning, August 19th, where it was discovered that several of the artillery horses were almost dead on their feet, but, after feed and a rest of three hours, they pushed on to Senatobia; arriving there, the men and horses were completely broken down. So Forrest remained all night, and moved early on the following morning. He learned that Hickahala creek was full with the banks, and it was necessary to bridge it in order to cross. But Forrest and his band of superhuman men were equal to any emergency. The writer several times heard General Forrest tell how he overcame the difficulty, and will give it in his own words as near as can be remembered.

Said he: "I had no idea of giving up my visit to Memphis, nor did I intend to lay around the creek waiting for it to fall. So I told Neely, Logwood, and McCulloch (Red Bob) to send their men to all the gin-houses for ten miles and bring in the flooring on their shoulders. There was a little narrow flat-boat not over twenty feet long on the north bank of the creek. Two of the men swam over and brought it to our side. I then set the men to work cutting grape-vines, which we twisted together, lapping them, until we had a long rope. I fastened one end to a tree, and sent some of the men over in the flat-boat to tie the other end. I used the flat-boat for my middle pontoon, and bundled together cedar telegraph poles I had cut down, which I used for the other pontoons. Before we got our pontoons in position, the boys began to arrive with the planks, which were put down as fast as could be, and by the time the last man was there with his plank, we were crossing the bridge. It did not require over three hours to build the bridge and cross, but I had to build a longer bridge over Coldwater river, where I again made use of the grape-vines for a cable. I found a lot of dry cypress logs, which we used in the same way we did the telegraph poles at Hickahala, and with the ferry boat for the middle pontoon, we soon made a bridge over Coldwater river, which we crossed in safety, and reached Hernando before night. I had to continually caution the men to keep quiet. They were making a regular corn shucking out of it. Wet and muddy, but full of life and ready for any thing. I never had greater confidence in them. Those were great soldiers."

When the command arrived at Hernando, General Forrest received information from his scouts, just returned from Memphis, that the city was quiet and without the slightest idea of the approach of a rebel force. He left Hernando, and rode all night (it was Saturday night), reaching near the vicinity of Memphis before daylight Sunday morning. The honest people and the thieves were all asleep, unmindful of the storm which hovered about them. The Federal soldiers had retired to their bunks without the least solicitude. They knew that General Smith was after Forrest, and if he did not capture him, he would keep him on the move. What had they to fear? They slept peacefully. No danger could possibly reach them. But how vain are all human ideas! Before reaching the pickets, Forrest halted his command, and gave the officers instructions. He explained comprehensively what each was expected to do. Captain W. H. Forrest, a younger brother of the general, was to take the advance and capture the pickets, after which he was to dash into the city and go directly to the Gayoso Hotel, where it was said General Hurlbut was quartered, as were also a number of other Federal officers. Colonel Neely, with the Second Missouri, Fourteenth Tennessee, and Eighteenth Mississippi, was to charge the camp in the outskirts, while Colonel Logwood was ordered to follow Captain Bill Forrest to the Gayoso with the Twelfth and Fifteenth Tennessee. Colonel Jesse Forrest, with the Sixteenth Tennessee, was instructed to dash through De Soto street to Union, and capture General Washburn and his staff. Colonel Bell, with Newsum's regiment and the Second Tennessee under Colonel Morton, also two pieces of artillery, was to be left on the outskirts as a reserve.

Captain William Forrest of all the men in our service was probably best fitted for the daring and desperate work assigned to him. He was a powerful man, five feet eleven inches tall, broad shoulders, weighing about two hundred pounds, and, like the general, a physical giant. He was brave to recklessness. He did not fear one man, nor did he fear a hundred men, and yet he was as sympathetic as a woman. He never provoked a quarrel, but, when disturbed, would shoot a man on the slightest provocation, and he would give the last cent he had to a person in distress. The writer has known him to do both. It has been often said that General Forrest never feared but one man, and that man was his brother William.

Every thing understood, Captain Forrest moved forward with ten picked men about fifty yards in advance of his company. He reached the picket about two miles out from the city, on what was known as the Hernando road, near where Trigg avenue crosses Mississippi avenue. As Captain Forrest rode along, the Yankee vidette heard the tramp of his horses, and called out quickly: "Halt! Who comes there?"

Captain Forrest answered: "A detachment with rebel prisoners."

The vidette replied: "Advance one."

Captain Forrest whispered to his men to follow closely behind him. They rode quietly up, and found a guard sitting on his horse in the middle of the road. It was just before daylight. As soon as Captain Forrest got within reach he struck the picket a deadly blow over the forehead with his heavy six shooter, knocking him off his horse. One of the men dismounted quickly and disarmed him. The others rushed at the picket guards, and captured them without firing a gun. General Forrest had cautioned every one to keep perfectly quiet. There was no noise. General

Forrest followed the advance closely, and about the time the pickets were made prisoners he rode up. Captain Forrest again moved forward and met the second guard, but unlike the vidette they fired at him, and ran for their lives. This circumstance excited our men, and simultaneously, though without orders, they dashed after the retreating Federals, and raised a yell. General Forrest, with his escort company, was close on their heels. He saw that the silence was broken, and that he could no longer conceal his presence. He told Gaus to blow the charge. At the first note of Gaus' bugle the regimental bugles responded with the charge, and before the first note ceased to reverberate the whole command raised a yell and lifted their horses off the ground.

No artist's brush will ever paint such a scene as that, and no pen will ever trace in words, language which can adequately describe it. Men who had been in the saddle for two days and nights wet and hungry, their horses worn out, now rushed over the enemy's camp yelling and shouting like flying devils. The Federals had no intimation that Forrest was near. They could not realize the situation. They must have thought the devils dropped out of the clouds. The wildest excitement spread in all directions. Captain Forrest with his gallant band of about forty men, depending entirely upon themselves, pressed forward, and ran into an artillery camp of six guns, caissons, horses, etc. They dashed on to the guns, killing or wounding nearly every man who exposed himself. This was near where the Kansas City, Memphis and Birmingham Railroad crosses Mississippi avenue. This little band pressed on to Beal street, crossed Main, and then to the Gayoso Hotel. Like avenging devils many of them rode their horses into the rotunda. The men rushed over the hotel, looking for General Hurlbut and other Federal officers. They created a panic equal to that at Pompeii when the city was destroyed by Vesuvius. Federal officers, suddenly aroused from sleep, ran from place to place *en deshabille*. Two of them, who did not realize the situation, began to curse the intruders, and made an effort to put them out. Those unfortunates were killed. Men and women screamed, the men were worse frightened than the women. The situation was inexplicable. It suggested the most awful and horrible thoughts that ever chased each other through the brain of man. People in the third and fourth story rooms heard the screams of those below, and the reports of two or three pistol shots. As they ran from place toplace, they asked: "What is it?" Very soon Captain Forrest's men were breaking open the doors. Officers hid under their beds and in the closets, but were dragged out. They begged for their lives. Big rough-looking men, coarsely appareled and covered with mud, a pistol in each hand, smashed in the doors, and were in full possession of the hotel. It was an awful situation to realize on getting out of bed. Those mud-covered men wanted General Hurlbut. He was not there, but he ought to have been there.

Many of the men who rode with Forrest into Memphis that August morning are living, and are good and local citizens of the Government of the United States. They are, in some instances, men of great prominence in affairs to-day. They are men of cultivation, refinement, influence, and wealth. They can be seen on the streets of Memphis any day, but a passerby would never suppose that those business-looking gentlemen, modest and unobtrusive, were the same daredevils who rode their horses into the rotuda of the Gayoso, ready to kill any Federal soldier who offered resistance, and who surprised and captured pickets and charged batteries. But such is a fact.

Captain Forrest, being in advance, aroused all the Federal forces. As soon as he passed and the officers caught their breath, they formed their men in line for defense. Colonel Logwood, who followed Captain Forrest, encountered a double line of infantry drawn up along the road not far from the artillery camp. Logwood was moving at a gallop. The first gray streaks of dawn were appearing, and the first intimation he had of their presence was a volley at the head of his column. Logwood was tempted to charge them, but he knew the importance of giving Captain Forrest support. Therefore he pushed on without halting. The enemy, greatly excited, shot over the heads of his men. As he reached Georgia street, Logwood found another line of infantry blocking his way. They opened fire, but at the head of the gallant Twelfth Tennessee, he led the charge against them.

The men raised a yell, and with guns in their right hands

raised above their heads, rode pell-mell over and beyond the line, scattering those who opposed and creating a panic. The Yankees dodged like squirrels. As he reached the point where Wellington street runs into Mississippi avenue, he discovered a company of artillery, and the men were hurriedly loading the pieces. There was not a moment to lose. His whole force would be shot to death in a minute more. But Logwood was the man for that occasion. With great presence of mind and courage, he dashed on the guns, and captured or killed the gunners before they could fire. He then rushed on to Hernando street, and by the old markethouse; then out Beal to Main, and to the Gayoso. As the men went rushing and yelling through the streets, the enemy fired at them from behind fences, from windows, and from house corners. But our men were wild. They dashed on without the faintest idea of danger; nothing but death could stop them. Numbers of our men had lived in Memphis, and were proud to see the city again. Women and men stuck their heads out of windows and doors, waiving sheets, dresses, and any thing they found handy. They recognized the muddy old Rebs, and welcomed them with all the enthusiasm in their power. Numbers of females, overcome by excitement, rushed out into the streets in their night-robes, forgetful of every thing except the present moment. They had, figuratively, left the earth and walked in the air.

Logwood and his gallant followers, after arriving at the Gayoso, renewed the search for Federal officers. He, however, posted a squad of men in each direction, to give notice of any advance of the enemy. After remaining in the vicinity until ten o'clock, he retired along Front street to Beal, and out to De Soto street. His scouts reported that the enemy was concentrating his forces, and would cut him off unless he moved quickly. Captain Forrest, with that recklessness and indifference to all opposition and danger which charaterized him at all times, decided to pay all his friends a visit. He was notified that the enemy on several streets was moving toward the Gayoso, but that made no difference to him. He had probably forty or fifty men. They mounted their horses in front of the hotel, formed company, and with Captain Forrest at the head, boldly rode through Gayoso street to

Main, and up Main to Union, as leisurely as if they had been south of the Tallahatchie. They turned into Union going east, and when about the middle of the block a column of Federal infantry turned column left out of Second street into Union. The Federal soldiers carried their guns at a trail arms, and moved at double-quick. The moment Forrest saw them, not over fifty yards away, he fired on them with his pistol, killing one of the men in the first set of fours. His men dashed on the column with such absolute recklessness they paralyzed them. As Captain Forrest rode toward them, he continued to shout: "Put down those guns!" The head of the Federal column wheeled to run without firing a gun, and coming in contact with those behind, caused great confusion. They knocked each other down. It might have been that those in the rear supposed that a large force of rebels was at hand. They ran with all their speed toward Gayoso street. Forrest's men continued to fire at them, killing and wounding several. Forrest did not follow them up, but continued his course out Union in a gallop, his men firing at every blue-coat they saw. The men hooted and yelled like Comanches. They reached De Soto street, and saw Colonel Logwood's column going south, and joined them.

Colonel Jesse Forrest, with his regiment, the Sixteenth Tennessee, had followed Colonel Logwood as far as Colonel Robert Looney's place, on Mississippi avenue, then ran through Lauderdale to Union and to General Washburne's headquarters. Unlike the other column, Colonel Forrest met with little resistance, but found to his great regret that General Washburne had escaped. He heard the firing on Logwood, and left the house, though Colonel Forrest captured the members of the staff who waited to put on their clothes before following their general's example.

General Forrest remained with the reserve under Colonel Bell. He knew an emergency might arise, in which case he wanted to be in a position to meet it. Colonel Neely, who had been ordered to attack the large infantry camp just south of Elmwood cemetery, was met by a terrific volley. The enemy heard firing and formed line before he reached them. This was unexpected, and checked Colonel Neely's gallant band. They, however, recovered, dismounted, and drove the enemy pell-mell. The enemy's force numbered over a thousand, while Colonel Neely mustered six hundred. General Forrest noticed the check Neely had received, and, quick as thought, called out: "Forward!" He dashed off to the east and right of the enemy, followed closely by his staff and escort, and Bell leading his command. It was General Forrest's intention to strike the enemy in the flank, but he passed near a cavalry camp, from which he was fired on. At no time or place during the war did General Forrest show to better advantage. There were several yard and garden fences intervening, over which he rode like a scythe over a wheat field. The cavalry, supposing the end of the world near at hand, fled in great confusion. He was riding old King Philip, before which no fence would stand. General Forrest rode several paces ahead, as usual. He held a long cavalry saber raised in his right hand, and looked more like a devil incarnate than any thing those Yankees ever saw. He was physically a large man, but on that occasion must have looked forty feet high, as King Philip mounted the fences. He captured one hundred horses and about sixty men. Colonel Neely, as above stated, dispersed the infantry in his front, who were joined by the dismounted cavalry which General Forrest drove off, all of whom took refuge in the State female college buildings, in which there were numerous windows that were used as port holes. General Forrest called on Lieutenant T. S. Sale, who commanded the section of artillery, to throw a few shells in the building, which he did with great celerity. The enemy, after reaching cover, opened a hot fire and defended the place with credit. General Forrest advanced a skirmish line, but concluded it would be too great a sacrifice to send his men against them; therefore, contented himself with watching Sale make holes in the wall and roof. It was the first chance Sale had on the trip, and he was anxious to batter the buildings, but General Forrest needed him for other work, and withdrew. Forrest, ascertaining that the enemy was massing his forces, having recovered from the shock, sent men into the city to collect stragglers and hurry them out to rejoin their commands. The commands under Colonels Logwood and Jesse Forrest, returning through De Soto street, to what is now Mississippi avenue, found a strong line of infantry, supporting a six-gun battery, just to the south of the Kansas City, Memphis and Birmingham Railroad, and extending across the Provine place. The force, as well as the guns, had full possession of the road, and commanded the approach from the city. That was a serious situation. Colonel Logwood sent Company "I," of the Fifteenth Tennessee, commanded by Captain Peter Williams, to take the battery. He charged at once, but was driven back. He recharged, however, reinforced by Company "H," also of the Fifteenth, commanded by Lieutenant J. M. Witherspoon, and captured the battery.

In the meantime Colonel Jesse Forrest had moved to the flank of the infantry, which frightened them off, leaving no enemy in front. The column quickly joined General Forrest, who, with Bell's and Neely's commands, was near the buildings where the enemy had sought shelter. It was now about noon, and General Forrest desired to retire, and let the pot stop boiling long enough to allow General Washburne to telegraph the situation at Memphis to Smith. Many of the men were dismounted, arranging such articles as they had captured on their saddles, when suddenly a long column of Federal cavalry was seen riding at a rapid gait in pursuit of a lot of twenty or thirty men, who had lingered in the city. General Forrest, ever quick as powder, knew what to do. It made him furious to see his men chased by such a large body. He wheeled King Philip in the road, and called on Colonel Chalmers with the Eighteenth Mississippi and Colonel McCulloch (Red Bob) with his Second Missouri to follow. He rode at the head of the great Second Missouri, with Colonel Red Bob by his side, to the right of the road, and sent Colonel Chalmers with his regiment to the left. They charged down on either side of the enemy's column, striking him right and left. It was a curious movement the enemy did not understand. It looked like spreading the wings of a partridge net to drive the birds through. They halted, and our stragglers galloped to their commands. The Federal officers acted with great courage, and tried to lead their men on, but could not do it. A Federal, Colonel Starr, seeing General Forrest, no doubt recognized him, and thinking to distinguish himself in a hand to hand fight, made a dash at the general. Colonel Starr did not live over ten minutes. He was no more in the hands of General Forrest than a butterfly would be in the claws of an eagle.

General Forrest, with some six hundred prisoners, and a large number of horses, then fell back, going in the direction whence he came. After going a short distance he had an opportunity to discover the character of his captives, and found that quite a number were unable to march, on account of having no shoes, while others were sick. He therefore sent a member of his staff, Lieutenant C. W. Anderson, back to the city with a flag of truce. He sent with him an officer, who was a member of General Washburne's staff, a prisoner. His instructions were to say to General Washburne that the prisoners in his possession were in a wretched condition, many of them without shoes or clothing, that he did not desire to see them suffer, and as an act of humanity he would propose to exchange them for such of his men as might be held as prisoners. Should General Washburne not have an equal number to exchange, he would parol the remainder. Should General Washburne reject the proposal, he would suggest then that he send clothing for his men. He would await General Washburne's pleasure at Nonconnah creek, about six miles from the city.

Lieutenant Anderson saw General Washburne, who said he had no authority to recognize the parol of the prisoners held by General Forrest, but would accept the proffered privilege of sending a supply of clothing. In a short time two Federal officers, Colonel W. P. Hepburne and Captain H. S. Lee, with a wagonload of clothing, were sent out. They reached General Forrest about 3 P.M., and the clothing was immediately distributed under direction of Colonel Hepburne. General Forrest then directed his surgeons to examine the prisoners, and such as were found to be sick and unfit to undergo the hardships of the march might be sent back with the wagon, but with the promise they would not bear arms against the Confederate cause, or in any way injure the cause, unless properly exchanged. About two hundred were turned loose on those conditions. The remainder, about four hundred, were mounted on the extra horses, and the march taken up to Hernando. Including the prisoners, General Forrest had about two thousand men without rations. He knew it would be impossible to obtain any thing before reaching Panola, therefore, with that promptness which always stood him in hand, he decided to make requisition on General Washburne. He wrote General Washburne, stating his inability to feed his prisoners, and suggested that inasmuch as he would not receive them on parole, that the least he could do would be to send them something that night. He stated he would encamp at Hernando. This communication was sent by Colonel Hepburne. About daylight the following morning, the same two officers reached the camp with two wagons well loaded with provisions. Rations were issued to the prisoners for two days, and there was ample left to feed our men also. General Forrest, desiring to impress General Washburne with the idea that he might renew his attack on Memphis, gave instructions to make the men as comfortable as possible for a few days. The Federal officers returned to Memphis, and as soon as they were out of sight, General Forrest moved rapidly to Panola.

Persons who heard the sharp call of the buglers on the morning just before daylight say it was the most awful and ringing sound they ever heard. No one except the men themselves knew what the situation was. People were left to depend entirely on imagination. Could it be that Gabriel was sounding the last call? The thunderous yells, the rush of the horses in the mud, the clanking of sabers and the rattle of spurs added to the awful situation. It was dark. Nothing could be seen. It had been said that the end of the world would come when no man expected it, and in the darkness of the night. Men and women asked themselves and each other if that was judgment day. They knew that war was cruel and spread desolation, but something worse than war was upon them. It was late for some of them to do so, but they prayed for their souls. They wondered if they would ever see the sunshine and the shadows again. Their brains were sizzing.

The caravan which Forrest escorted out of Memphis, Sunday afternoon, August 21, 1864, was in deep distress. The children of Israel, whom Moses led across the Red Sea, dry shod, were no more downcast and discouraged before the passage than was that lot of Federal prisoners. Moses' crowd had probably sufficient clothing, but those poor fellows were in an exceedingly bad condition. Some of them had on nothing but their underclothes, while others had nothing but night-shirts. Great numbers of them had no hats, and very few of them had shoes. Officers who had pranced about the streets of Memphis in their gay uniforms, in some instances doing duty as staff officers, mounted on good horses with elegant saddles, were now in a sad and pitiable plight, as they trudged along in the mud, their gowns wet and draggling. There was no merriment or humor in that party, and the old "Johnnies" felt too much sympathy for them to indulge in any levity. Terrible stories were told after the raid into Memphis of how Forrest and his men acted. A number of people anxious to appear as heroes told ridiculous tales of what they passed through. One of the best stories told was by a Negro soldier, who claimed to have seen General Forrest as he rode up to the front of the Gayoso Hotel. He described to his companions how Forrest looked and the size of his horse. Said he: "I was er stanning right in dis alley when I seed him came up. He rid his hoss right up to de hotel, and I'm telling you the Gord's truf, he hitched his hoss right to the second story bannisters. I seed him. I seed him."

And there are to-day old Negroes in Memphis who can show you where he hitched his horse. The Negro's idea was that he was as big as "Colossus of Rhodes."

CHAPTER TWENTY-ONE

General Chalmers' Movement Against Memphis –
The Regiment of State Troops – Pleasant Stay at
Bolivar, Tennessee – Arrival at Paris Landing –
The Undine and Cheeseman Captured – First
Confederate Flag Seen Afloat – Ten Million Dollars
Worth of Property Destroyed in One Engagement
on the Tennessee River – Official Confirmation –
Brilliant Work of the Artillery

General Forrest arrived at Grenada, August 24, 1864, and in a few days set about to reorganize his forces. In the meantime, General Chalmers with that Spartan band, which so successfully resisted the advance of General Smith and completely concealed the absence of General Forrest, fell back to the south bank of the Yocona river, and went into camp at Springdale. Too much praise can not be given to General Chalmers for his brave, bold, wise and persistent generalship on that campaign. Confronted by a finely equipped army of twenty-two thousand men, he disposed his forces in the most advantageous manner. It was important that he should not be drawn into an engagement, and yet it was necessary to keep constantly in front of the enemy, harrassing them in every way, engaging Smith's attention, and keeping from him the information that General Forrest had gone in the direction of Memphis. General Chalmers' force numbered about thirty-three hundred men, but he deployed them so skillfully General Smith believed ten thousand men were in his front. The attack he made on the Federal lines on August the 19th, at Hurricane Creek, was sharp and brilliant, and it established forever the characters of his men. Wet and hungry, knowing the great disparity in numbers and equipment, they did not hesitate. The attack startled General Smith. He felt sure fresh troops were at hand, which made him exceedingly cautious. General Forrest in the reorganization placed the troops of each State together. Chalmers' division was composed of two brigades: the first, commanded by McCulloch (who had recovered from his wounds) composed of the Second Missouri, Lieutenant-Colonel R. A. McCulloch; Willis' Texas Battalion, Lieutenant-Colonel Theo Willis; Seventh Mississippi, Lieutenant-Colonel S. M. Haynes; Fifth Mississippi, Colonel W. G. Henderson; Eighth Mississippi, Colonel W. L. Duff; Eighteenth Mississippi, Colonel A. H. Chalmers. The second, commanded by Colonel E. W. Rucker, consisted of Forrest's old regiment, Lieuenant-Colonel D. C. Kelly; Seventh Tennessee, Colonel W. L. Duckworth; Fourteenth Tennessee, Colonel J. J. Neely; Fifteenth Tennessee, Colonel F. M. Stewart; Twelfth Tennessee, Lieutenant-Colonel J. M. Green.

Buford's division was also composed of two brigades: one commanded by Colonel E. T. Bell, the other by Brigadier General H. B. Lyon; the former being Tennessee, and the latter Kentucky troops.

On the 29th of August, General Chalmers was ordered to West Point, Mississippi, General Maury having called for assistance. McCulloch's brigade reached West Point, September 3d, and went at once by rail to Mobile, and we were deprived of the services of that splendid command until after the Nashville campaign. Before any other troops got away General Maury telegraphed that the necessity for help had passed, and General Forrest at once began preparations for a raid in the rear of Sherman's army. He left Verona with all the best troops in the command on September 16th, and moved in the direction of Florence, Alabama. He attacked and captured a number of block houses, and destroyed large quantities of stores. General Chalmers was ordered to Grenada to take command of all dismounted troops, and such cavalry as could be gotten together in the State, and was expected to defend the country against any movement from Memphis. He was advised by Henderson's scouts that the enemy was making extensive preparations to leave Memphis. He was well aware that he could not check a movement of that kind, and on October 5th moved north with about one thousand five hundred men, poorly equipped, to prevent the raid if possible. We marched rapidly toward Memphis. The enemy had every thing in readiness to begin the movement south, but advised of Chalmers' aggressiveness, deemed it safer to remain at Memphis and defend it. General Forrest was being pressed in West Tennessee, and this demonstration prevented troops going against him, which were now held awaiting the outcome of Chalmers' movement. The army at Memphis destroyed the bridges on all the approaches from the south and east, and dug deep ditches across the roads and streets. Breast-works were hurriedly thrown up, and the greatest alarm took possession of the garrison. They believed that Chalmers had a large force and intended to attack the city. Skirmishers were sent out to drive the enemy's pickets in. We remained in the neighborhood of Nonconnah all day, then moved to the east of the city, as if seeking an easier or better point of attack. In this way the enemy was at a loss to understand the objects of the expedition, and while they were thus deceived General Forrest made his return to Jackson safely. Arriving at the latter place he telegraphed General Chalmers to join him. This order was received at Como, and the march was begun at once toward Jackson. Among the troops General Chalmers had gotten together, on his bold and highly successful demonstration against Memphis, was a regiment of Mississippi State troops, composed of boys twelve to fourteen and old men sixty to seventy-five years of age. They volunteered in answer to a call made by Governor Pettus. It will be remembered that each farmer in the Confederacy gave the government ten per cent of his crops, which was designated "Tax in Kind." A mischievous rascal of Chalmers' regular troops seeing a little boy with an old squirrel rifle nearly twice as long as its owner was tall, asked him if he was Tax in Kind. The idea was taken up at once, and the State troops were called ever afterward "Tax in Kind" by the regular troops.

Just after going into camp the first night near Memphis, the colonel of the "Tax in Kind" regiment approached General Chalmers, and asked: "Are we not in the State of Tennessee?"

"Yes," replied the general, "this is Shelby county, Tennessee."

"Well, sir," said the colonel, "my men volunteered to defend Mississippi. You would not allow us to bring any cooking utensils, and we have no bread; therefore, I shall return to Mississippi."

The general knew his point was well taken, but it was necessary to retain the regiment for a few days. He said: "Colonel, let us talk about it;" and they walked to the general's campfire. The general's purpose was to treat the colonel so hospitably he could not well afford to withdraw his regiment.

Arriving at the fire, he said: "Jim, get to work. I have invited Colonel to take supper with me. Give us the best you have."

Jim punched up the fire and made his preparations. He stirred up his dough in a bucket, got a few corn shucks, which, after saturating, he filled with the dough, then covered them in hot ashes. He then sliced some fat bacon, which he broiled over the coals on the end of a stick. The colonel observed the utensils used, and while Jim was preparing supper, the general recited the story of the "Alamo." He told of the one hundred and seventy-two patriots under Colonel Travis; how they resisted the attack of Santa Anna with his three thousand Mexicans, and when it became apparent to Colonel Travis that all hope had departed, he announced the fact, saying: "I will die like a man for my country;" and with his sword he made a line on the floor, and called on those who were willing to make the sacrifice for freedom to cross it.

"And do you know," continued General Chalmers, "they all crossed to Travis but one. His name was Rose." The general was eloquent. About one hundred boys who had listened to the story clapped their hands. Just at this time Jim announced that supper was ready, and he handed to each of us an ash-cake the shape of an ear of corn and a slice of bacon.

The colonel ate a bite or two, then said: "General, I see the point. I can stand it if you can, and if my boys are willing, we will stay."

The boys, with one accord, said: "Stay, colonel, stay." And they did stay.

We arrived at Bolivar, October 16, 1864. General Chalmers was invited to make his headquarters at the home of Mrs. Thomas McNeal. His family and the McNeal family had been friends for many years. It was an elegant home, surrounded by beautiful shrubbery and flowers. The house was large and well ordered, and Mrs. McNeal presided with an ease and grace which is unusual in this day. Before the war she entertained distinguished people. Mr. McNeal was a nephew of President Polk, and the latter was often a guest at this charming Southern place during his life. Mrs. McNeal was well qualified for the duty of hostess, having had the advantage of a thorough education and extensive travel. She was descended from a long line of ancestors whose homes had been noted for open and unstinted hospitality, where the most cultivated people gathered to enjoy music and bright conversation and all the pleasures of refined society. But there was another feature about that household which attracted the attention of the staff, particularly the young members. Miss Irene McNeal, though not yet grown, was the embodiment of the highest promises of girlhood. She was at that age when the world smiled on her, and she returned smile for smile in the most gentle, graceful, and happy manner. She was bright and witty, and as beautiful as a bird of Paradise. Of the staff, Crump, Lindsay, Mills, Taylor, and Bleecker were unmarried, and if the Federals could have captured our forces as readily as those gentlemen capitulated to the charms of this young lady, the war would have ended in a short time.

We smile as we look back on those scenes. Neither of the boys had encouragement to suppose that the little queen was partial to him, or to either of them, but that greatest of all blessings, "hope," conquered reason and they lived in the future.

We spent a week most delightfully, and all regretted when the time came to leave. Before bidding good-bye to that beautiful home, it may not be inappropriate to say that Miss McNeal was not captured on that occasion. She is now Mrs. Jerome Hill, of St. Louis, and retains her charms to a remarkable degree.

The entire command by this time had reached the vicinity of Jackson, where it remained a week, resting the horses. On October 24, 1864, General Buford was ordered to Huntingdon, and General Chalmers to McLemoresville. Colonel Rucker resumed command of his brigade, having recovered from the wounds received at Harrisburg, while General Mabry commanded the Second Brigade of Chalmers' division. When General Buford reached Huntingdon, orders awaited him to proceed at once to the mouth of the Big Sandy and blockade the Tennessee river; and with Lyon's brigade he went direct to Fort Heiman, leaving Bell's brigade at Paris Landing. There is a long straight stretch of river in each direction at both places, which enabled General Buford to observe any movement of the boats. He had Walton's two twenty-pound Parrott guns commanded by Lieutenant Willis O. Hunter, at Fort Heiman, and a section of Morton's battery at Paris Landing. General Chalmers, having arrived at Paris, was ordered to move at once to Paris Landing with Rucker's brigade and a section each of Walton's and Rice's batteries. We left Paris just before the dawn of day, and arrived at Paris Landing, a distance of twenty-two miles, about 11 o'clock A.M., October 30th. Here we learned that General Buford had captured a steamboat, the *Mazeppa*, loaded with army supplies of all kinds. Also, that a gun-boat and steamboat had attempted to pass Fort Heiman, that General Buford had fired on them, and at that time both were anchored at the bend of the river between the fort and Paris Landing. When the *Mazeppa* was deserted by her crew, she rested against the opposite shore; we had no means of crossing the river, but a gallant fellow of Walton's battery, Dick Clinton, plunged into the river and soon stood on deck. He tumbled a skiff overboard and went back for General Buford, and when the prize was brought to our bank, the general was standing on deck with a demijohn in his hands. Saluting the crowd on shore, he said: "Rations and clothes for the boys and whiskey for the general."

The gun-boat, which was the *Undine*, began shelling Bell's

position, and this was the situation when General Chalmers reached Paris Landing. There was a long open shed at the landing, behind which Bell's brigade had fallen back from the river into the woods to get out of reach of the *Undine*'s shells. General Mabry's brigade and Thrall's battery were left at Paris. General Chalmers and Colonel Rucker, with their respective staffs and escorts, reached Paris Landing some twenty minutes ahead of the brigade, where they found shells bursting and making a terrific noise, and topping the trees. They were joined by Colonel Bell, who explained the situation.

General Chalmers said: "Gentlemen, I think we can silence that machine, provided we can get our guns in proper position," and turning said to Colonel Rucker, "Ride down the river and see what you think about it, I will be governed by your judgment." Colonel Rucker returned in a short time, and said: "General, I can take Walton's two ten pound Parrots and a regiment and capture or destroy both boats." He was then ordered to do so, and with the two guns mentioned, which were under the immediate command of Sergeant Crozier, and Logwood's and Kelly's regiments, moved quickly to position. He planted the Parrotts just above the boats, and dismounting the men sent them under the command of Colonel Kelly to a point just below the boats, with instructions to fire into the port holes and at the pilot house. The first shot from the Parrotts was a signal. As soon as Rucker opened, the *Undine* moved to the other shore, for the purpose of getting into better position. She could not elevate her guns sufficiently to do him any harm from the position he found her in. The armament of the *Undine* consisted of eight beautiful brass pieces. She fired broadside after broadside, but Rucker filled her so full of shot and shell that the crew, who were not disabled, took to the woods.

Colonel Rucker ordered Colonel Kelly to take possession of both the *Venus* and the *Undine*, and proceed with them to Paris Landing. In the meantime, General Chalmers dismounted the balance of Rucker's brigade, and moved them under the bluff to the water's edge. He posted a section of Rice's battery under Lieutenant Briggs just above the landing, some three hundred yards off. Very soon a steamboat hove in sight coming down the river. She proved to be the *J. W. Cheeseman*, and was loaded with a lot of sutler's stores, pickles, coffee, canned goods, etc. The men were ordered to keep quiet. She rode the river as gracefully as a swan. The men were restless and hard to restrain. They had no idea of allowing her to escape. On she came, and just after passing Briggs' position he opened fire on her. The first shot fired passed entirely through the cabin. The crew made for the hull. The engineer shut off the steam, and the boat turned crosswise the river. As she approached the landing a yellow Negro boy wearing a white cap stood leaning over the guard. He was enjoying the fresh air, and dreaming of the future, wholly unmindful of any danger. But when the first shell from Briggs' guns struck the boat he disappeared. After the smoke and splinters had cleared away he was gone. That is all we ever knew of him. In a few minutes a white flag was sent up from the hatchway, and a moment later the firing had ceased.

General Chalmers called out: "Come to the landing."

The answer was shouted back: "The wheel is broken, we can not manage her."

He then said: "Send a boat and a rope." Soon a yawl was lowered, and two men with one end of a rope in it pulled for our shore. The other end was fastened to the boat. Our men were in a hilarious mood, and crowded down near the edge of the water. No child ever anticipated more happiness, nor expected so many beautiful things would come to him on Christmas, than did the men of Rucker's brigade expect to gather when the *Cheeseman* should land. General Chalmers decided to protect the office and cabin from a general spoliation, therefore, ordered a detail from his escort company to report to Lieutenant Bleecker, who would board the steamer as soon as she touched the shore, and guard the passage at the head of the stairway. Frank M. Norfleet and Oliver D. Sledge reported for service. When the yawl reached the shore a hundred or more men soon took the rope and began to pull. The gang plank was projecting over the bow of the steamer as she neared shore. Frank Norfleet was the first man aboard, closely followed by Lieutenant Bleecker and Oliver Sledge. Before the plank reached the shore Captain Wm. Tucker, who was anxious to be first on board, made a jump, but slipped and fell into the river. He swam ashore, wet, but wiser. The boys were soon at the head of the steps, while the men began to crowd on the boat. It was remarkable how quickly the boat was stripped of every thing worth moving. Barrels of pickles, hams, coffee, etc., lined the bank. Neither Delmonico nor Mme. Begue ever prepared a spread that gave as much pleasure as the men had that night. Bleecker and his two companions found nothing in the office or the cabin worth mentioning, and so advised General Chalmers. Then they began the hunt for happiness. It is said that "music hath charms to sooth the savage breast," that art and poetry inspire the mind of man, but for a rebel soldier a lot of "grub" was superior to every thing else.

Soon after the *Cheeseman* had been captured, another gun-boat was seen coming down the river with a chip on her shoulder. The officers evidently believed they would soon drive us away. She came to anchor about a mile off, and began to throw her shells. The distance was too great for Briggs' gun to be effective against her; therefore General Chalmers directed him to move nearer, which he did, and drove the gun-boat away. At this stage of the game it looked very much as if we owned the Tennessee river.

General Forrest reached us on the morning of October 31st. He was greatly pleased with the success of the expedition, and decided at once to have the damage to the boats repaired, and go into the fleet business himself. It was ascertained that Briggs had irreparably ruined the *Cheeseman*, so she was burned. But the *Venus* and the *Undine* were placed in order. Walton's two twenty-pound Parrotts were put on the *Venus*, under command of Lieutenant W. O. Hunter, and she was made the flagship, with Lieutenant Colonel W. A. Dawson in command. Captain Gracy was given command of the *Undine*. The Fourteenth Tennessee was detailed as a crew, and with Confederate flags flying from both vessels, they started on a trial trip to Fort Heiman. It was the first time in our lives we had ever seen a Confederate flag on a boat. The men ran along the bank for a mile, waving their hats and cheering. The boats returned to Paris Landing without accident, and on the morning of November 1st we started up the river to Johnsonville. General Chalmers was ordered to keep near and support the fleet. We camped that night on the bank of the river. It soon began to rain, and poured all night.

Next morning, bright and early, we set out again. We reached a bend of the river, where our boats got ahead of us. No sooner done than three gunboats began firing on them. A shot struck the *Venus*, disabling her. Captain Dawson then ran ashore and abandoned her. Walton, Moulton, and Rice ran their guns in position and forced the gunboats to retire. We soon came in sight of Johnsonville, where our gun-boat was attacked both from above and below. Several gun-boats followed us from the south, and, in conjunction with the three at Johnsonville, made it so hot for the *Undine* that Captain Gracy and his men ran her ashore and set fire to her. We lost our big twenty-pound Parrotts when the *Venus* was captured. We moved forward, and found General Mabry, with Thrall's battery, in position about two miles below Johnsonville. He had been sent there direct from Paris by General Forrest. The following morning, Mabry took position opposite Johnsonville, supporting Thrall's battery. Excavations were made in the ground, and Thrall's guns placed in them. General Lyon, with about four or five hundred men, joined us, and he, with a section of Walton's battery, was stationed above Mabry. Rucker was opposite Johnsonville, just below Mabry. He had Morton's battery, sunk also in the same way. Rice's battery and the other section of Walton's were below. The horses were all moved back into the woods, and the men found protection behind logs and trees.

General Forrest directed that the attack should begin at 2 P.M., November 4th. General Chalmers was to give the signal by a rifle-shot. He sat near the water's edge with a Springfield rifle, and at the appointed time took aim at the pilot on a steamer. Lieutenant Bleecker sat beside him, and saw the glass break just to the right of the pilot's head. He was a good marksman. Immediately all our guns opened, Thrall's first. General Chalmers and

Bleecker retained their positions and watched the effect of the shells. It was a great surprise to the enemy, who thought our forces had left the neighborhood. The batteries from the land opened a terrific fire on our position, as did also one of the gun boats. The big shells crashed and tore through the woods, limbing and smashing the trees. The enemy had a large quantity of supplies piled up, covering about two acres of ground. Men were seen walking about, some loading the steamboats, others merely looking on. The second shot from Thrall's battery exploded the boiler of one of the gun-boats. We could hear the people scream as the steam enveloped them. Gunners jumped through the port-holes into the river to escape the burning steam, and were drowned. A moment later, a shot from the same battery exploded a magazine, setting the gunboat on fire, and the flames were swept down against the others, and these too were soon enveloped in a fiery sheet. This circumstance excited our gunners, who began to land the shells in the boats rapidly. Very soon every vessel was burning. Men jumped in the river. The panic was frightful. Those on the boats would run from one end to the other, then despair and jump in the river, to drown. Within two hours, we had burned four gun-boats, eleven steamboats, and twenty barges, besides all the stores on shore. The Federal accounts afterward stated the loss at ten million dollars. By night, every thing on the Johnsonville side was a mass of ashes.

The following morning we took up the march; Rucker, with his brigade and Morton's battery, were the last to leave. Just as he was leaving, a regiment of Negro troops, supposing our command all gone, came out from cover, rushed to the bluff, and began cursing the rebels, daring them to come back and give them a chance. Nothing on earth could have suited Colonel Rucker and Captain Morton better than to accommodate the blood-thirsty Negroes. He ordered the guns in position and moved his brigade to the bluff. The fire from the battery was followed by the deadly rifles of the cavalry. The Negroes ran in the wildest confusion without firing a gun. Numbers of them were killed and wounded. After that brief interruption, Rucker followed Chalmers with his command. The affair at Johnsonville was a remarkable success. We destroyed about ten million dollars worth of property, and killed and wounded a large number of the enemy, while our loss was the two twenty-pound Parrotts, two men killed, and four wounded; the Parrott guns being lost on board the *Venus*, when she was sunk by Colonel Dawson to avoid capture.

The following report, made by General Chalmers four days subsequent to the engagement, was found in the War Department Records by a friend, and handed me after the above was written. It is a paper of great value, and confirms the recollections of the writer almost entirely. Of course, no one could give so complete a report to-day as one written at the time, and which was official, and, too, by so able and intelligent an officer as General Chalmers. It will be noticed that General Chalmers speaks several times of Hudson's battery in his report. When the company was formed it was called "The Pettus Flying Artillery." The captain, Alfred Hudson, was killed at Shiloh. Soon after the battery had been given to General Forrest, Lieutenant E. S. Walton was made captain, and commanded the company until the war closed. The battery was always called Walton's Battery by the command:

> Report of Brigadier-General James R. Chalmers, C. S. Army, Commanding Cavalry Division
>
> Headquarters Chalmers' Division, Forrest's Cavalry,
> Perryville, Tenn., November 8, 1864.
> Major – In obedience to orders from Major-General Forrest, commanding, etc., I moved, on the morning of the 30th of October, from Paris, Tenn., with Rucker's brigade, my escort battalion, and four pieces of rifled artillery (one section of Rice's and one of Hudson's battery), to Paris Landing, on the Tennessee river, where I arrived about 11 A.M. on the same day. I found Colonel Bell at the landing, with his brigade, of Buford's division, and a section of Morton's battery. He reported to me that a short time before my arrival a gun-boat and two transports had passed his position, going down the river, and that, in obedience to orders from General Buford, he had reserved his fire until they had passed, and had then opened upon them, and he thought had

done them some damage. One of the transports succeeded, as I was afterward informed in passing Fort Heiman, where General Buford was stationed with the Kentucky brigade of his division, a section of Morton's battery, and the two twenty-pound Parrott guns of Hudson's battery, but was badly crippled in the attempt. The other transport (the *Venus*) and the gun-boat (the U. S. Steamer *Undine*, No. 55) were at the bend of the river about midway between the positions of Colonel Bell and General Buford, and out of range of the guns of either. After a consultation with Colonel Bell, I directed him to move his artillery down the river to a point as nearly as possible opposite to the boats, and to drive them from their position. He rode off to reconnoiter, and, on returning, reported that the order could not be executed on account of the ground to be passed over. My artillery having arrived, was placed in position on the bank of the river, above that held by Colonel Bell, with an interval of several yards between the sections.

Colonel Rucker, coming upon the field, suggested that the guns should be moved down the river to attack the boats, and on being told that Colonel Bell had reported the ground impracticable for artillery, he proposed that he and I should re-examine it. We accordingly rode down the river, Colonel Bell accompanying us, but before we had found a suitable position, a courier reported another transport coming down, and Colonel Bell and I returned to the batteries, leaving Colonel Rucker with orders to continue his reconnaissance. The transport proved to be the *J. W. Cheeseman*, a stern wheel steamer. She was allowed to pass the upper battery (Rice's) unmolested, but as soon as she came opposite to the middle battery (Hudson's), the guns of both opened upon her, and her steam-pipe was cut and other parts of her machinery disabled. As she was passing Hudson's battery, Colonel Bell's battery also opened upon her, and a heavy fire of small arms being poured into her by troops stationed along the bank of the river, she was soon compelled to surrender. Soon after this, Colonel Bell moved his brigade to Fort Heiman in obedience to orders from General Buford, whom I had directed to consolidate his division at that point.

Colonel Rucker having reported that he had found a practicable route and a good position for attacking the boats below the landing, I directed him to move down to it with the section of Hudson's battery (two ten-pounder Parrott guns), the Fifteenth Regiment and Twenty-sixth Battalion Tennessee Cavalry of his brigade, and attack them, which he did with such vigor and success that after a severe artillery duel between his battery and the gun-boat, the latter was disabled and driven to the opposite bank, where all of her officers and crew, who were able to do so, abandoned her and escaped, leaving only the dead and wounded behind.

At the same time, Lieutenant-Colonel Kelly, commanding the Twenty-sixth Battalion Tennessee Cavalry, attacked the transport *Venus*, which was defended by a small detachment of United States Infantry, so sharply that she surrendered to him, and the gallant colonel, going on board of her with two companies of his battalion, crossed the river, took possession of the gun-boat, and brought both safely to the landing. While this fight was going on, another gun-boat (the *No. 29*) appeared above us, and coming to anchor about a mile and a half above our batteries, began to shell them. The upper battery (Rice's) returned a few shots, but finding that the distance was too great for effective firing, I directed it to move up nearer to the boat and ordered a portion of my escort battalion and the cadet company of the Seventh Alabama Cavalry to support the battery and act as sharpshooters. After a brief and spirited engagement, the gun-boat weighed anchor and withdrew up the river. The *Cheeseman* was so badly injured that it was impossible to repair her with the means at our command, and she was afterwards burned by order of the major-general commanding, as were also the three barges captured on the same day. The transport, *Venus*, and the gun-boat, *Undine*, being only slightly injured, were soon put in repair by his order. These boats being bound down stream, after having delivered their cargoes of freight for the United States government at Johnsonville, contained no stores beyond the usual supplies for their own use and a small quantity of private freight of but little value for army use. The *Undine* belonged to the class of gunboats known as "tin clads," and was one of the largest boats of her class on the river. She carried eight twenty-four pounder brass howitzers, and when captured had all of her armament and equipment on board of her.... An attempt had been made to spike two of the guns and to disable one by placing a shell in its muzzle, but these were soon removed.

I have been more minute than may seem to be necessary in giving the particulars of the capture of these boats, because I am aware that some dispute has arisen as to what troops are entitled to the honor of their capture. I do not regard this as a matter of much importance, since all that was done was but the execution of the plans of the major-general commanding, and whatever honor may arise therefrom is due first to him who conceived and then to those who executed them. All of the troops, so far as I am informed, acquitted themselves well, but I feel it is but just to those who took the most prominent part in the execution of those plans that they should receive the greater share of that honor which is the dearest reward of the soldier. I repeat, therefore, that when the *Cheeseman* was captured, there were six guns playing upon her, of which two (of Morton's battery) belonged to Colonel Bell's command, and four (two of Rice's and two of Hudson's battery) belonged to my command. They were placed on the bank of the river, Rice's being the upper, Hudson's the center, and Morton's the lower battery, and the boat was disabled before she had passed the center battery by one of the first shots fired at her.

The gun-boat, *Undine*, and the transport, *Venus*, were captured after Colonel Bell had withdrawn his brigade, including his artillery, and when there were no troops present excepting those belonging to this division. The troops immediately engaged in the capture were the Fifteenth Regiment and the Twenty-sixth Battalion Tennessee Cavalry, and one section of Hudson's battery. It has been said, however, that these boats were badly crippled by Colonel Bell as they passed his position in the morning and before any part of this division had arrived, but in reply to this I would respectfully say that the *Venus* was not materially injured when she was captured, as is shown by the fact that she was used immediately afterward to tow the gun-boat to the landing. The shot which struck her injured her cabin and upper works, but had not damaged either her machinery or hull. Colonel Bell stated to me that, in obedience to orders, he did not fire at either of the boats until they had passed his position. This exposed their sterns and larboard sides to his fire, but the shot which disabled the *Undine* struck her in front and on the starboard side and could not have come from Colonel Bell's battery. In addition to this, the boat was manageable and maintained a sharp fight for some time after Colonel Bell had withdrawn his brigade. In view of these circumstances, I think it evident that the greater share of the honor of capturing these boats belongs to those troops to whom they were actually surrendered.

Our loss in this affair was one man of Rucker's brigade severely wounded. That of the enemy, so far as we have been able to ascertain it, was five killed and six wounded on the Venus, three killed and four wounded on the *Undine*, and one wounded on the *Cheeseman*. Total, eight killed and eleven wounded. We also captured forty-three prisoners, among whom was one officer and ten men of the United States infantry. The others belonged to different boats.

On the morning of November 1st, I moved my command up the river as far as Danville, where we encamped, placing our guns in position on the river bank so as to protect our boats (the *Undine* and *Venus*), which had been ordered to move up the river, keeping in rear of our batteries. On the following morning, I moved toward Reynoldsburg, in accordance with previous instructions, but was afterward ordered by the major-general commanding to halt near Davidson's Ferry and to place my guns in position at that place, which was done. Our boats having ventured too far beyond the protection of our batteries, were attacked by two of the enemy's gun-boats, and the *Venus* was recaptured by them. On the 3d inst., we moved up the river opposite to Reynoldsburg and Johnsonville, and had frequent skirmishes during the day with the enemy's gun-boats, of which there were three at the latter place, but without any decisive results. Here we were joined by Colonel Mabry's brigade of cavalry, and Thrall's battery of twelve-pound howitzers, attached to this division, which had been left at Paris, and had moved directly from that place and taken position a short distance above Johnsonville. On the 4th inst., General Buford having come up with his division and Morton's battery, the latter was ordered to the position occupied by Colonel Rucker, and my division was formed as follows: Colonel Mabry, with his brigade and Thrall's battery, on the right, immediately above and opposite to Johnsonville; Colonel Rucker, with Morton's battery, and the Seventh Alabama Cavalry, immediately below and opposite to that place; Lieutenant-Colonel Kelly, with the Twenty-sixth Tennessee battalion and two guns of Rice's battery, opposite to Reynoldsburg;

and Lieutenant Colonel Logwood, of the Fifteenth Tennessee Cavalry, with his regiment and a section of Hudson's battery, at Clark's house, still further down the river, and about two miles below Johnsonville.

The enemy had at Johnsonville three gun-boats and a number of transports and barges, variously estimated at from eight to ten of the former and from twelve to fifteen of the latter – some of them laden, together with an immense quantity of government stores, a part of which was contained in a large warehouse, and the remainder piled upon the bank, covering about an acre of ground. The town was defended by a strong earth-work, well garrisoned and supplied with artillery, and they possessed an additional advantage in the fact that the bank of the river on that side is much higher than that on which we were.

At two P.M. the bombardment began, and in a short time one of the gun-boats was set on fire. One after another, the others followed, and before nightfall all of the gun-boats, transports, and barges, the warehouse, and the greater part of the stores on the shore, were set on fire and consumed. The enemy kept up a heavy fire from their gun-boats and land batteries until the former were disabled, but without inflicting any serious injury upon us, or forcing any part of our troops to abandon their position. During the engagement, five gun-boats came up the river, evidently with the intention of reinforcing the town, but they retired after a sharp cannonading with the artillery under Colonel Logwood's command.

Our loss in this engagement was very small, but as the official reports have not been received, it can not now be stated with accuracy. All the officers and men under my command deserve honorable mention for the very creditable manner in which they have borne themselves during the entire expedition, and I do not desire to detract in the slightest degree from the honor due to the others in calling especial attention to the gallant conduct of the Seventh Alabama Cavalry in this their first engagement, and to the very effective service rendered by Thrall's battery in setting fire to the enemy's boats and stores.

My thanks are due to the officers of my staff, and to Captain Lawler, Seventh Tennessee Cavalry, and Lieutenant D.F. Holland, aide-de-camp to Major-General D.H. Maury, who were temporarily on staff duty with me, for their efficient services.

I am, major, very respectfully, your obedient servant,

Jas. R. Chalmers, *Brigadier-General.*
Major J.P. Strange, *Asst. Adjt.-General, Forrest's Cavalry.*

Before leaving Mississippi, General Chalmers gave orders to Colonel R.F. Looney and Captain A.D. Bright to go into West Tennessee, in the neighborhood of Memphis and points north thereof, for the purpose of arresting and bringing into our lines such deserters and stragglers as could be found. These gentlemen were selected for the duty because of their familiarity with the country, and further because they were known to be men of nerve. They left the command at Como, and went direct to the house of Captain A.J. Hays, near Arlington, where they remained a few days perfecting their plans, and greatly enjoying the hospitality of that elegant home and family. While sitting at the dinner table one day, soon after arriving at Captain Hays', a Negro boy ran into the hall, crying out: "The Yankees are coming in the front gate." Colonel Looney and Bright had no hope of escape except by getting out the back way, which they proceeded to do with all the speed in their power. Bright, though a very large man, was exceedingly quick and active, and as strong as a horse. They managed to get into a corn field, and then separated, going in different directions. The enemy, however, followed on horseback, and fired on them as they went. A large Dutchman, mounted on a good horse in pursuit of Bright, called on him to halt. He exhausted the charges in his rifle, and began to curse, saying: "Halt, you d—n rebel! Do you think you can outrun a race horse?" Of course, the Dutchman's horse finally overtook Bright, and he was forced to surrender. The Dutchman again said: "You d—n rebel, you can run like a deer! You must be used to it."

Both Bright and Looney were made prisoners and carried to Memphis. They reached Germantown, and were turned over to Colonel Lee, of the "Kansas Jayhawkers," who escorted them into the city on the following day. On the trip from Germantown, the gentlemen had nothing better to do than to make a good impression on the "Jay hawker," and by the time they arrived at Memphis had prevailed on him to let them go to the Gayoso Hotel. Information of their capture had preceded them, however, and when they reached the hotel, they were met by an orderly, who advised Colonel Lee that General Hurlbut desired the prisoners sent to his official headquarters, which were on Madison street, in the building now occupied by the *Commercial-Appeal*. Arriving there, they found Major Bob Sanford and four other officers, who were also prisoners. An officer of General Hurlbut's staff (said to have been one of the most arrogant, impudent, and discourteous men in the army) greeted them by saying: "I think I can tame you chaps." Then, addressing the guard, said: "Put them in close confinement; they will be held as hostages! The rebel general, Tilghman, has sentenced a number of Federal soldiers to be executed, and if he carries out his threat, we will kill each of these" (pointing to the seven Confederate officers before him).

They were then hustled down the stairway and over to the "Irving Block Prison," on Second street, between Court and Jefferson. They were placed in a back room and strongly guarded, but in a short time the officer ordered that they be moved to the third story, a dirty place, where thieves, thugs, and cut-throats were kept, and where vermin abounded. It was a serious situation, but Colonel Looney was not the man to submit to such indignities, even in the face of death, and therefore protested against it. He used strong language to the officer in charge, and denounced the action as an outrage. The officer admitted it was unusual to associate officers and gentlemen with the third story prisoners, but said: "I understand you seven men will be shot, and it is necessary to take extra precaution to prevent your escape. I am ordered to see that nothing interferes with the proceedings." The gentlemen realized that unless something in the way of a miracle occurred their time on earth was of short duration. There was not a bed of any description in the long room, neither was there a chair or bench to sit on. They walked the floor all night.

About sunrise the following morning Colonel Looney was standing at a window looking out on Court square, thinking doubtless of his once happy childhood, and the pleasant days spent in the little park before him, as compared to his present con-

dition. Major Sanford, Captain Bright and the others were leaning against the begrimed walls, thinking of the horrors that seemed to await them. Colonel Looney saw a wagon approach and halt just opposite and below the window. It contained seven rough pine coffins, and one of them was much larger than the others. He was interested, of course, and deeply so, in ascertaining why the wagon halted in front of the window. H
demic in the city, therefore, seven coffins in one wagon was an unusual sight, but the colonel had remarkable nerve, and did not succumb to the dismal outlook. He called to Captain Bright to come over, and pointing out the wagon, said: "Bright, look! There are seven of them, and I suppose the big one is for you."

Bright looked the colonel full in the face and said: "Colonel Looney, you should not joke on facts, they make me shudder," and then returned to his corner in the dark and dirty room.

About eight o'clock, Judge Nooe passed along the street, and Colonel Looney called to him, saying: "Do you understand the awful situation we are in? Try and do something for us. See Doctor Fowlkes and any others you can, and bring them up to see us quickly."

Very soon four or five citizens called on General Hurlbut, and made an earnest prayer for the lives of the Confederate officers. In the meantime, one of the guards informed Colonel Looney that the seven coffins had been placed in the hall-way of the prison. About 10 o'clock, A. M., Colonel Sam. P. Walker (father of the present Judge S. P. Walker), Judge Nooe, Doctor Fowlkes, and a few others, called to see the gentlemen, and said: "Your friends are earnestly working, and hoping to save you from death by agreeing to accept for you life sentences in the penitentiary at Alton."

About four o'clock in the afternoon they were removed from the Irving Block to Fort Pickering, guarded by twenty or thirty soldiers. Nothing further had been said about a commutation of the death sentence, and as they looked out of the window and watched the flow of the great Mississippi river, noting the bluff where, according to tradition, De Soto stood when he first beheld it, the future presented nothing but gloom and sadness. It was an ideal spot for an execution, and while they remained in the fort they had time to consider and discuss among themselves what was best to do with the few hours yet left to them.

The following afternoon, about four o'clock, an officer announced to Colonel Looney that he was wanted in the city. As he walked to the gate he saw a carriage standing there. Into this he was told to go, and then surrounded by guards on horseback, and with two armed men sitting opposite him, was driven toward the city, and halted on Shelby street, at a house where he met Colonel Walker, Dr. Fowlkes, and his own brother Dave (the latter having come down from Paducah.) They advised him that a number of prominent gentlemen had tendered General Hurlbut a banquet that evening, on which occasion they hoped to obtain his consent to exchange them for some Federal officers, prisoners at Jackson, Mississippi. They believed it could be accomplished, and wanted the gentlemen to know what their hopes were, and what steps were being taken for their safety. Colonel Looney was returned to Fort Pickering, and gave the cheerful news to his comrades. The following morning, Colonel Walker, Dr. Fowlkes and Judge Nooe called to say that General Hurlbut had consented to let them go, provided an equal number of Federal officers of similar rank were released. But that in the event this could not be accomplished then they should return to Memphis as prisoners, and on those conditions they were escorted to the picket lines and turned adrift, and the seven men who had been so near the brink of all earthly hopes were free again. While bidding the officer of the guard good-bye, Bright wanted to know what would become of the seven coffins, now that they were released. Said the officer: "We will give you yours, if you want it." But the polite offer was respectfully declined, with thanks.

CHAPTER TWENTY-TWO

The Effort to Cross the Tennessee River at Perryville – Forrest and Chalmers Build Boats, Cross the River at Florence, Alabama – Wagons and Negroes Captured – A Dutch Officer Bested By a Negro – Desperate Charge at Henryville – The Great Mistake at Spring Hill – The Battle of Franklin – Arrival at Vicinity of Nashville

We reached Perryville and found General Forrest building a ferry-boat. There were a few vacant store-houses, which he tore down for the material. He had his staff officers and escort company carrying plank and scantling on their shoulders down to the river. The general was ripping off weather-boarding with his own hands, and "guying" the members of his staff because they did not carry better loads. General Chalmers with his staff and escort was the next to reach Perryville. He learned from General Forrest what his purpose was, and decided to try his skill in building a boat also. He called on us to get to work. It was very muddy. Some of the staff and several of the escort who usually wore tolerably good clothes made very wry faces, but all hands were soon busy, and within two hours our boat was riding the waters, not as gracefully as a swan, but as proudly. It was arranged to begin the crossing early on the morning of November the 7th, but we soon discovered that our boats were unsafe, and they were abandoned. The wagon train reached us about nine o'clock with two large yawls, which Colonel Rucker had taken from the *Venus*. These were used by the men to cross, and the horses were made to swim. The river was rising rapidly, and a quantity of driftwood in the river made it dangerous. So, after crossing the Seventh Tennessee and Kelly's regiment (about four hundred as good men as ever answered roll-call), General Forrest decided to abandon any further effort on Perryville. He gave Colonel Rucker orders to move to Mount Pleasant, and report to General Hood. We bade the boys good-bye with some apprehensions, but we knew if any four hundred men in the world could take care of themselves, Rucker and his men could.

We moved to Florence, Alabama, via Iuka; the roads were as muddy as could be, and it continued to rain day and night. Our horses were broken down for want of food. General Forrest gave instructions to send men out along the line of march and exchange the broken down horses for fresh ones, but there were none to be had. The artillery made slow headway. Finally General Chalmers found a lot of oxen, which he used for the artillery, and we reached Iuka, November 13th, after the most disagreeable march we ever had. We rested two days, and left Iuka on the 16th, and on the afternoon of the 17th, reached Florence, where we found General Hood's army encamped. Hood's men cheered us as we passed along. They had heard nothing but good reports of Forrest's cavalry. We crossed the river on a pontoon bridge, and went into camp on Shoal creek, distant about two and one-half miles. General Hood was detained at Florence awaiting supplies, and the nearest railroad station to Florence was Cherokee, sixteen miles, between which points the roads were almost impassable. It would seem, therefore, that the movement to Nashville was a failure before the army crossed the river. It was a desperate condition, however, which confronted the Confederate cause, and nothing was left but desperate chances. This fact was well known to our men, and yet they were ready to move forward, and to do every thing in their power to change the current of events.

Early on the morning of November the 18th, our command moved toward Henryville, Tennessee, followed by the wagons which contained all we had, together with several of our Negroes. General Chalmers with his staff and escort bringing up the rear an hour later. We had gone about a mile, when it was discovered that our plunder was scattered along the road and in the woods. We followed the trail in a gallop. It was evident that the enemy had captured the wagons and possibly the troops. General Chalmers determined to find out. We passed empty wagons locked against trees, and other evidences of a hasty retreat. It was a rough, rocky country. Finally we came in sight of the enemy with our mules, drivers, and Negroes. They had lost the direction, and were returning on the same trail they went. As we rode to the top of a hill, and started down, the enemy was coming down an opposite hill meeting us. General Chalmers was mad. He called out: "Charge them! Charge them!" We raised a yell and began firing at them. The enemy was about four hundred strong, but they had lost hope, and ran in every direction. The escort rushed at them, and succeeded in capturing nearly all, together with our mules and Negroes.

Major Mills had a very handsome little sorrel horse which Boston was leading when captured. He had a sore back. When Boston recognized us, and saw the "Yanks" running, he almost went wild with joy. After quiet was restored, and the prisoners stood corralled, prior to marching off, Boston began in a very loud voice to tell how it all came about. He was not gifted with intellect, nor with extraordinary oratorical power, yet he made a reputation that day as a talker. Finally he caught sight of a big fat Dutchman with sergeant's stripes on his arms, and he went at him with the fury of a panther. He said: "You! You! You! wus de berry ole Dutch Yankee whut tuck Mars Andrew's filly." He snatched the Dutchman's hat (a nice felt one), and began to kick him, and no doubt would have injured him but for the intervention of Captain Goodman, who made him behave.

We captured about three hundred prisoners and horses. The escort company and some of the staff exchanged their broken-down horses for the fresh ones, and after some delay all the plunder was gathered together, and the wagons proceeded on the journey. The enemy's force was a scouting party, sent out to discover our position, and by accident fell in behind us. The escort boys were heroes. Sixty-five men charged and killed or captured over three hundred, without the loss of a man. We reached a little place called West Point, and remained there until the 23d of November, when Colonel Rucker joined us, and we had great rejoicing at finding the boys all right. We moved on the 23d to Henryville, Rucker in advance. He met a cavalry force about an hour before night, some two thousand strong, which he attacked at once. Generals Forrest and Chalmers joined him in a short time. Our force was less than a thousand men. The balance of Rucker's brigade was some five miles in the rear. General Forrest ordered Colonel Kelly to take his regiment to the left of the pike, and attack the enemy in the rear, while with his escort company he went to the right. General Chalmers remained with Rucker, and pressed the enemy back gradually. General Forrest soon struck his rear with his escort company, and created a panic. It was just getting dark, and the enemy were filing into the woods to go into camp. They did not think we were mean enough to continue the fight after night. General Forrest dashed through their ranks, and scattered them in great confusion. The force which General Chalmers was fighting, hearing the firing in their rear, retreated. General Forrest, with his escort concealed on the side of the road, poured a deadly volley into them as they passed, killing about sixty, and creating the wildest stampede. In the meantime, Chalmers and Rucker, hearing the firing, and noting the panic, charged in column, the men yelling like Indians, driving or capturing every thing before them. The darkness made it awful for the enemy.

The following morning, Rucker again took the advance, and caught the rear of the enemy about half way between Mount Pleasant and Columbia. He drove them beyond a creek near Columbia, where they took cover behind breastworks. In the last charge on that day, November 24th, Colonel W. A. Dawson was killed. We saw his body lying beside the pike as we followed Rucker. He was a gallant officer.

General Scofield, with an army of twenty-two thousand infantry, and eight thousand cavalry, was strongly intrenched at Columbia. His force was equal to General Hood's. We drove his pickets in on the 25th, and could see their lines of battle awaiting us. General Chalmers made his headquarters at General Lucius Polk's, from which place we rode out on the morning of the 26th, and found that Colonel Rucker had advanced his line some three hundred yards, driving the enemy from his outer rail works. There was a mill by the pike, where Generals S. D. Lee, Forrest, and Chalmers went to take observations from the second story. They noticed the enemy moving to cut Rucker off, and General Chalmers directed Bleecker to see him quickly, and tell him to fall back to his original position. Bleecker rode off, passing through an orchard, where the enemy's shells were clipping off limbs, and plowing up the ground. He reached Colonel Rucker, who was some distance in front of his line, and delivered the order, and started on his return, when a grapeshot struck the pummel of his saddle and shattered it. The shot passed within one inch of his body, but that fact did not trouble him so much as the loss of his fine "Texas saddle."

Walton's battery in the meantime was giving the enemy much annoyance. It was in position about half a mile to the left of the mill, throwing shell into the enemy's works. Walton was a splendid officer, young, brave, and dashing. He was probably one of the best shots in the artillery service, and could often, after a few trials, put his shells wherever he chose. General Chalmers, with the aid of a glass, discovered that Walton was landing shells very successfully, and suggested a ride over to his position. Generals S. D. Lee, Forrest, and himself, followed by their staff officers, soon reached Walton, who was enjoying the work fully as much as a boy does playing "sweep-stakes." We were there but a few minutes when the enemy, no doubt thinking the thing had gone far enough, opened on Walton with thirty or forty guns. The earth trembled. Probably a hundred big shells exploded above us in less than half a minute, fragments flying in all directions. A caisson was blown up at the same time, making the explosion terrible. After the smoke had partially cleared away, we saw General Lee sitting on his horse, calm and motionless, not in the slightest degree excited, while the rest of us, including General Forrest, were on the ground, and several of the horses gone. We were not long in getting away from there. Fully half of Walton's horses were killed before he could get under cover. General Chalmers said afterward, that when he saw General Lee so undisturbed, he felt ashamed, but on finding General Forrest off of his horse, and hearing him say, "Get away from here," he thought he could stand it.

A moment before the shell from the enemy's gun struck the caisson, Corporal John T. Moore was squatting in rear of the limber chest, cutting the fuse of a shell for one of the guns. He was interested in getting the exact time for the fuse, when the explosion occurred. Moore was thrown high in the air and fell upon his back, badly bruised and his clothing torn into shreds. He was wearing a long gray blanket overcoat, which was wrecked. After regaining his feet, pointing to the scraps of coat, he said: "That d—n Yankee has destroyed my coat."

We spent the night at the beautiful home of General Lucius Polk, whose kindness, hospitality, and liberality will never be forgotten as long as there is one of us left. He was a grand man and a worthy representative of that distinguished class which has nearly become extinct. During the night of the 27th, General Schofield crossed his army to the north bank of Duck river. General Forrest, acting under orders from General Hood, sent General Chalmers with his division to cross seven miles above Columbia, at what was called the "Cedars." General Buford crossed below, while General W. H. Jackson crossed still higher up than General Chalmers did. We made the passage without special incident, and moved along slowly for four or five miles, through a rugged and rocky woods. General Forrest sent an officer to General Chalmers, saying that General Buford had met with stubborn resistance, and as yet had not been able to cross the river. We then went into bivouac, and early next morning received orders to press the enemy's cavalry, and, if possible, get in their rear. We had gone but a short distance when our advance found them in line, but they were nervous.

Captain Bill Tucker was commanding what we called the escort battalion, composed of Raines' company, the escort company, and two other unattached companies. When our advance guard began firing, General Chalmers ordered Captain Tucker to charge. There were a number of cedar trees which had been blown down, probably years before, the limbs of which were as hard and as strong as a buck's horn. Tucker was a gallant fellow. He was brave to recklessness. As he rode by at the head of the battalion, General Chalmers said: "Captain Tucker, break that line." His boys responded beautifully. They went sailing through the woods, yelling at the top of their voices. Tucker rode a very handsome horse, which belonged to his brother, Fenton, called "Duff Green." He was known by nearly all the men in the division, because of his style and gaits. Several of the escort rode abreast of Tucker. They were high-strung, spirited fellows, who would not permit Tucker to lead, and no man could lead Tucker. On they rode with the fury of lightning, firing their pistols as they went. There was a large cedar tree before them, the limbs pointing in our direction. Tucker, heedless of every thing, expected Duff Green to clear it, but that was impossible. He made the effort, when a sharp-pointed limb caught him and passed entirely through, killing him. Tucker was soon mounted on another horse, and went at them again. The enemy gave way, but we had continuous fighting through the day, reaching Spring Hill about four in the afternoon.

Several of those gallant boys of the escort company were afterward killed, and a few only survive to-day. Among those living are: Frank M. Norfleet, of Memphis; Oliver D. Sledge, of Como, Mississippi; Dr. Tom M. Jones, of Hernando; and D. W. Wagner and T. J. McFarland, of Water Valley, Mississippi.

Our men had been fighting on foot almost continuously during the day, and the country over which we passed was rugged and thickly covered with stubby cedar trees and bushes. Therefore, the command was out of ammunition and broken down. At Spring Hill we found a cavalry force in line of battle, which Colonel Rucker easily dispersed, but they retired behind a long line of breast-works, which were filled with a corps of infantry. Rucker withdrew and reported the fact to General Chalmers, when they both rode forward to investigate further, and found as Colonel Rucker had stated. Very soon the enemy's stragglers began to pass along, and from those captured we ascertained that fully as many more infantry, besides artillery, were on the march from Columbia to Spring Hill. It was plain, therefore, that we were in the rear of the enemy.

    This was the situation when General Forrest rode up, but in the meantime about two hundred of the enemy's cavalry had returned to the position from which General Rucker had driven them, and General Forrest, observing them, said to General Chalmers: "Why don't you drive those fellows off?"

    General Chalmers answered: "Why, there are three divisions of infantry in breast-works behind the cavalry, and, further, my men are out of ammunition and broken down."

    Said General Forrest: "I think you are mistaken; that is only a small cavalry force. I will lend you Wilson's regiment, which, together with your escort company, will drive them away."

    General Chalmers felt that he could not argue the matter further, so said: "All right; let me have Wilson; I will try it."

    Soon the line was formed, with the general and his staff and escort on the right. He gave the command, "forward, gallop," and immediately Carson sounded the charge. The escort began to yell, and Wilson's men took it up. We charged through a beautiful grove, the men urging their horses. General Chalmers was leading, and they were determined to be with him. General Forrest watched the charge, which also put the men on their mettle, and there was not a laggard in the line. We had almost reached the edge of the woods when the shock came. Twenty pieces of artillery opened upon us, followed by the fire of a long line of infantry. Horses tumbled over each other, and fell, men were shot, and horses galloped away riderless, and limbs and bark covered the ground. It was a dreadful few minutes, and it all happened very quickly. There was no command given to fall back, but when the smoke rose above there were only four men in their places: General Chalmers, Lieutenant Elbert Oliver, of Raine's company, Frank M. Norfleet, and Carson, the bugler. They were together, but the next moment Oliver and Carson were shot down.

    Then Norfleet said: "General, every body but you and me

have been killed or wounded; let us get away," and they rode to the rear. After getting out of range, General Chalmers and Norfleet halted, and, returning to the command, met General Forrest, who said: "General Chalmers, you were right. They were there."

"Yes," replied General Chalmers, "that is the second time I found them there."

Soon General Buford reached us with his division, and he and Generals Forrest and Chalmers made a reconnaissance. Returning, General Forrest ordered the line forward for a demonstration. We could not make an attack because both divisions were out of ammunition. Chalmers was on the right, and, every thing ready, we moved forward, driving the enemy's skirmishers, who withdrew to the breast-works. We remained in that position but a short time, when Cheatham's corps came up. General Cleburne was the first infantry officer to arrive. He formed his division on our left, and we charged with him. It was well understood that our command had no ammunition, and the only thing we could do was to yell. General Cleburne was riding a tall bay horse, and presented a very soldierly appearance. The enemy could not stand the onslaught, and fell back from the works they were in to another and stronger line. By this time it was nearly night, and we retired to feed our horses and get ammunition, while Cleburne held the position he had gained.

Soon the firing ceased, and General Cleburne rode back, I presume, for orders. Meeting General Chalmers, he remarked: "They are badly paralyzed. I rode within fifty yards of their works without danger." At that moment blood tricked out of a wound in his horse's neck. As we rode to camp, we met Brown's division, of Cheatham's corps, standing in column. The writer heard a conversation between Generals Brown and Chalmers on the situation. General Chalmers said: "I believe that, if you will join General Cleburne, and make a vigorous attack, you can capture or rout the force in his front."

General Brown replied: "I have no orders."

General Chalmers said: "I would make the attack without orders, general. I am confident it is a great opportunity; the enemy is very uneasy, and could be whipped and captured before the balance of Schofield's army can come to his assistance."

General Brown answered: "I will await orders."

There was a nice large residence in the suburbs, which we passed when we arrived at Spring Hill. We rode there hoping to get something to eat, and met General Forrest and his staff. Our horses were fed in the yard, and we sat around on the gallery. About nine o'clock an officer of General Forrest's escort reported that General Cleburne had withdrawn his command, and that the enemy was moving toward Franklin. General Forrest then mounted his horse and went in person to see General Hood (whom we understood had his headquarters about a mile distant) and advised him fully of the situation. It was said at that time that General Hood stated to General Forrest that General Cheatham's corps held possession of the turnpike, but General Forrest assured him that such was not the case. General Hood then asked General Forrest if he could not quickly obstruct the pike, and prevent the enemy's retreat until he could get Cheatham in position. General Forrest replied that Chalmers and Buford were out of ammunition, but that General W. H. Jackson would do every thing in his power to check the retreat. General Hood assured General Forrest that his corps commander would supply Chalmers and Buford at once with ammunition, but this was not done until the following morning, when General Walthall furnished twenty rounds of ammunition to the man. The ordnance wagons had not yet reached us, and no more could be obtained.

During the night of November 29th, at Spring Hill, General Schofield's army passed along the pike in sight of our camp without any interference. Numbers of stragglers left the line of march to stop at our camp fires. They were entirely ignorant of the fact that we were in their rear. The greatest opportunity ever presented to an army to capture or annihilate an opposing army was neglected at Spring Hill. The advance corps of General Schofield's army, which we found at Spring Hill, separated some six or eight miles from the balance of his command, was in a panicky condition, and there is no doubt had the divisions of Cleburne and Brown been thrown against them the army would have surrendered. There was great disappointment at that time, and a certain officer was severely criticised, but nothing has been written concerning the responsibility since, and the writer will pass it by.

It must be recognized that General Hood displayed much shrewdness and ability in getting to the rear of General Schofield. It was a masterly move, and somebody was responsible for not winning a great victory. We left Spring Hill about 9 A.M., and crossed over to Carter's creek turnpike, going toward Franklin, which place we reached about 2:30, P.M. We were the first troops to arrive, and constituted the extreme left of the army. Our advance guard encountered and drove the enemy's pickets to a stone fence, where they made a stand, but the Seventh Tennessee moved forward and drove them back into their breast-works. Very soon we could see our army arriving. Groups of officers on horseback were halted on top of the hill overlooking the town, taking observations and receiving orders. General Forrest with Buford's and Jackson's divisions was on the right of the enemy, therefore General Chalmers reported directly to General Hood. From our position we could see three lines of breast-works encircling the town, and each line was full of infantry and artillery. General Chalmers sent his adjutant general, Captain Goodman, to see General Hood, and explain the situation and ask for orders. Captain Goodman returned with orders to charge the enemy at once. General Chalmers, believing that General Hood did not understand the strength of the enemy in his front, sent Lieutenant Bleecker to him, with additional information of the enemy's force and position, and he received the same or similar answer.

When Bleecker reached General Hood he heard him say to General Cheatham: "Get your men in position, and bring on the fight," or something to that effect.

General Cheatham turned to several general officers in the group and said: "You hear the order," and General Brown repeated the same thing to his brigadiers, "You hear the order." Immediately they all galloped off in the direction of their respective commands, and soon the brigades were moving in columns of regiments down the hill and toward the enemy. Bleecker noticed a young man with a brigadier's uniform on and asked Captain Wigfall, of General Hood's staff, who he was. Said he, "That is General Gordon."

"No," said Bleecker, "I have often seen General Gordon with the Army of Northern Virginia; that is not he."

"But," said Wigfall, "that is George W. Gordon of Tennessee." He was mounted on a very handsome iron-gray horse, and looked every inch an ideal soldier. Bleecker watched him as he rode away. He was a superb horseman, and wore a bright new uniform and sword. Bleecker was particularly attracted by his youthfulness, and was anxious to see him under fire. As he rode back to General Chalmers with the orders he saw General Gordon form his line, then dismount and take position on foot in front of his brigade. In a few moments he advanced, and became obscured by the smoke of battle.

If hell be more terrifying than the scenes of the six or seven hours which followed the one above described on the hill overlooking Franklin, on the afternoon of November 30, 1864, then I abjure mankind to halt and consider. General Chalmers charged across a cornfield, and drove the enemy from his first line of works, which we then occupied, and from which we continued a desultory firing until the enemy began to retreat, about one A.M. To our right the fighting was hot and fast. Great clouds of smoke overhung both lines, and we could only see the continued flashes of the guns. Our troops were at a great disadvantage. They could not use the artillery, because it would have demolished the city of Franklin and killed her noble and patriotic women. The enemy's artillery was used with terrible effect. Shells went crashing and shrieking through the air, and smashing and bounding over and into the ground, oftentimes exploding under the ground, and throwing up great mountains of earth. The air was filled with a whizzing blare, and after night came on the scene was sublimely and awfully grand. The shells could be followed by the burning fuses, which flashed and twittered like thousands of skyrockets, and when they burst all the sizzling sounds of hell could be heard. There was no music in them, and only those who have heard the wicked things have any conception of their shrill and dreadful noise. Hundreds of these horrible shells were fired at us every few minutes for five hours. It looked as if the devil had full possession of the earth.

When Cleburne's and Brown's divisions moved forward, they charged across an open field and drove the enemy from the first line of earthworks, and followed him closely into the inner works. In that fearful struggle, hundreds of brave men gave up their lives. These were men who had served from the beginning, and had suffered through the campaigns of Bragg and Joe Johnson, but they fought with fierce energy, and threw themselves against the enemy's works with the madness of despair. Every color-bearer was shot down, and each succeeding hero who dared to raise them was killed. It is impossible to exaggerate the conduct of the Confederates at Franklin. Of the twelve generals whom Bleecker saw in conference with General Hood just prior to the attack, five were killed, three wounded, and one captured. General John Adams, on horseback, leading his men, bounded over the enemy's works, and grasped the flag of the Sixty-fifth Illinois regiment and bore it to the ground. Was there ever a more gallant deed? He knew full well it was a sacrifice of his life, but he did not hesitate. He and his noble steed died side by side at the same instant. And the gallant, devoted, and chivalrous Cleburne was killed not more than fifty yards from the enemy's works, as was also Generals Cranberry, of the famous Texas brigade, Strahl and Gist, of Cheatham's corps, while Generals Cockrell, Quarls, and Brown were wounded.

Bleecker's hero, General George W. Gordon, followed the enemy into his last works, where his men and those of the enemy fought with such desperation that Gordon's command was almost annihilated. They were within five feet of each other. Nothing but a bank of earth divided them. The enemy's position on both the right and the left enabled him, therefore, to enfilade Gordon's line. It was madness to continue the struggle, and some of Gordon's men attempted to retreat, every one of whom were killed. Finally others called out to the enemy that they would surrender, and they crawled over the bank, leaving General Gordon and a few men who were near him. The enemy's fire was so deadly that the few left protected themselves behind the bodies of their dead comrades. But, except General Gordon and two others, those few men were soon killed, and he then gave his white handkerchief to one of the two, who tied it on his bayonet and raised it above the works. The surrender was accepted, but as they stepped down into the ditch, a "beast" wearing a Federal uniform made a vicious strike at General Gordon's head with the butt of his gun. A Federal officer partially warded off the blow and saved his life, but he received a painful wound on the shoulder.

We revere the memories of the distinguished dead, the privates not less than the generals. The men who gave up their lives at Franklin on the Confederate side were martyrs to a hopeless cause. They felt regret at the lost opportunity at Spring Hill (not their fault), and went blindly forth to retrieve the errors, and were willing to redeem the mistakes of their officers with their lives, if necessary. We can not overestimate their noble and heroic deeds. Every American citizen should feel a pride in cherishing the memory of the gallant men who stormed the works at Franklin, as well as those who defended them. There are some who participated in that dreadful battle living, but history will never do justice to their bravery, trials, and sufferings, and on the roll of honor among the living, none deserve more admiration and respect than the modest and chivalrous gentleman whom Memphis feels proud to claim, in the person of General Geo. W. Gordon.

When daylight dawned on Franklin, Tennnessee, December 1, 1864, the scene was indescribable. About five thousand Confederates and two thousand Federals lay dead or wounded in and around the Federal breast-works. In many instances, Confederates and Federals lay across each other, and there was one case where a Confederate and a Federal were found dead in the ditch, the Confederate grasping the Federal's throat. Notwithstanding General Schofield retreated about 2 A.M., leaving his dead and wounded in our hands, our army was badly whipped. The men knew that no earthly good had been accomplished, and that the flower of the army had fallen. They had hoped for brilliant results in Tennessee, but met disaster. They could never again look into the faces of the noble men, the pride and glory of so many battles, who lay dead upon the field at Franklin, and their hearts were filled with gloom and sorrow. And this was the condition of Hood's army as it moved toward Nashville. During the night, Bleecker's horse was killed, but Colonel McGavock, a distinguished citizen of Franklin, presented him with a fine colt, a four-year-old thoroughbred, and which had never before been saddled. Colonel McGavock had two Negroes to assist in putting the saddle and bridle on, and then Bleecker mounted. The colt stood on his hind legs first, then on his front. He reared and ripped and plunged all around the lot. The Negroes ran into the barn, and the boys of the escort looked on from the outside and laughed. There seemed to be no end of the colt's ambition to throw Bleecker off, but he finally quieted down and fell in with the escort company and became a cavalry horse.

The night of December 1st, we arrived at the hospitable home of Colonel John Overton, where we remained until the following morning. It was a typical "Southern gentleman's palace," situated in a beautiful grove, surrounded by well-cultivated acres, fine orchards, herds of thoroughbred cattle, a stable of blooded horses, and a retinue of trained servants; and we were royally received and charmingly entertained. Miss White May, a most accomplished and patriotic young lady, a member of Colonel Overton's family, contributed very much to our pleasure, and won the admiration and esteem of General Chalmers and his staff. Our chief surgeon, Dr. G.W. Henderson, a gentleman of the most accomplished manners, who had the highest appreciation of ladies of almost any man the writer ever knew, expressed to Miss May, upon our leaving the next day, the great happiness he felt, and assured her that he would never forget the visit to her home. The doctor, I am sure, made a favorable and pleasant impression on the family. He was a good conversationalist, a talent inherited, no doubt, from his distinguished ancestor, Chief-Justice Henderson, of North Carolina. Bleecker and the doctor were the last to leave, and they were both willing to surrender, but circumstances would not permit. They finally said good-bye and rode toward the "big gate." The doctor had loaned one of his pistols to a friend, and the remaining one kept him busy keeping his holster in place on the front of his saddle. They had gone about fifty yards, when the holster, to which was attached his halter-rein, fell to the ground, and the horse, becoming frightened, made a sudden bound, turning the saddle and throwing the doctor off. Bleecker was greatly alarmed for the safety of his friend, but the fiery colt which he was riding began to plunge, and he was unable to dismount for some minutes. Miss White May and Mrs. Overton, seeing the doctor on the ground, and supposing he was dangerously hurt, ran as rapidly as they could to his assistance. The doctor gained a sitting posture, but his back being toward the house, he did not see the ladies approaching, and just as they came within speaking distance, he began to curse his horse for being such a d— fool. Then, turning his head, he saw the ladies, sprang to his feet, and begged pardon for his hasty words. The ladies made no reply, but with sincere concern urged him to return to the house. He assured them he was not hurt, and soon we were galloping on to catch the command. After going some distance, they halted, when the doctor asked Bleecker if he remembered what he said, because it was very certain the ladies heard him, and he was deeply grieved. He declared he would never swear again, and told Bleecker he must never speak of the circumstance to any one. Said he: "The thought of the d— old horse throwing me in the presence of ladies!"

We reached the vicinity of Nashville, and General Chalmers was invited to make his headquarters at historic "Belle Meade," the home of General W. G. Harding. We occupied all that portion of the line extending from the Harding pike to the Cumberland river. Each morning we rode out to the line and returned about four in the afternoon for dinner. On December 6th, General Hood notified General Chalmers that General Stewart would relieve him on the Harding pike, and that he could move his troops at once to the Charlotte pike near the river, and orders were sent to Colonel Rucker accordingly, and he withdrew. When we reached the line we found a brigade of infantry (Ector's) standing in column. Soon General Stewart rode up, and asked about the distance to the picket line. General Chalmers answered that his force had been relieved, that he had no pickets on the Harding pike, and suggested that a line be advanced at once.

General Stewart then requested General Chalmers to send out a squad to locate the enemy's lines. He called on Bleecker to take five men from the escort company and do this. Bleecker selected D.R. Wagner, W.J. Hughes, F.M. Norfleet, J.T. West, and W.G. Robinson. There was a heavy fog that morning which prevented them from seeing distinctly more than thirty yards beyond them. They rode on about half a mile, and suddenly came in sight of a fire on the side of the pike and heard men talking. Bleecker halted, and called on Dan Wagner to go forward with him to ascertain whether they were friends or foes, and left the other four to await developments. Bleecker was riding the highstrung McGavock colt, and proceeded cautiously to within twenty yards of the fire before they were discovered, when a man said: "Look there! Look there!" and quickly a considerable squad began firing. Bleecker and his party wheeled and ran. They went racing down the pike, and the enemy continued to fire, but fortunately neither of them was hurt. Bleecker discovered that he had a great horse, which ran easily ahead of the others, but when he wanted to halt, that was another question. He neared the point where Generals Stewart and Chalmers were, and began to pull his rein, but the colt went bounding on like a frightened deer. He ran fully half a mile before he stopped, and when he returned General Chalmers had moved on. He did not find him again during the day. All the boys wanted the McGavock colt.

    General Forrest, with Buford's and Jackson's divisions, was at Murfreesboro, and remained in that vicinity until after the disaster at Nashville.

Lieut. Bleeker, Aug. 1864

CHAPTER TWENTY-THREE
The Battle of Nashville – Very Cold Weather –
Hundreds of Men Barefooted – General
Chalmers' Gallant Fight at Davidson's Landing –
Colonel Rucker's Personal Fight and Capture –
General Forrest Saves the Army –
Recross the Tennessee River

On the 9th of December, the weather became very cold, and a heavy fall of snow was followed by sleet. The infantry suffered very greatly. Many of them were without shoes, and had very scant clothing, but, fortunately, there was little or no fighting; therefore, they could remain by the fires when not on duty. During that awful weather, General Chalmers and his staff were the guests at "Belle Meade," the hospitable home of General Harding. Mrs. Harding was a lady of marked character and ability. She presided over that grand old home with unsurpassed elegance, and I venture to speak for all the party, when I say they were never better or more hospitably entertained. General Harding had two daughters. The eldest, Miss Seline, barely grown, while the other, Miss Mary, was scarcely more than a child, and yet she was capable of entertaining the most intelligent men of the party. They were both very patriotic and loyal to the cause, but Miss Seline was enthusiastic. Dr. Henderson would tell Bleecker, after they retired at night, about his hunt for human happiness. Said he: "I have at last found it. Here is a man with vast estates, surrounded by all the comforts and luxuries which the most cultivated mind can suggest, an accomplished wife and lovely daughters; what else can he desire?" The doctor employed the choicest rhetoric in speaking of Miss Seline. He thought she was the most beautiful and interesting girl he had ever met, and that was the opinion also of the others.

One night during the inclement weather, Mrs. Harding made a large bowl of snow cream. The doctor was very fond of it, and she gave him a smaller bowl to take to our room. After eating what we wanted, he placed the bowl on the window-sill outside of the blind, and cautioned Bleecker not to open the blind for fear of knocking it off. The general had given instructions for an early start the following morning. The curtains in our room were closely drawn, and the blinds being closed, we did not awake until Captain Goodman walked into the room, calling on us to get up. The doctor sprang out of bed and threw open the blinds to see how late it was. Of course, it was the very window in which he left the snow cream, and the bowl was thrown to the stone walk below. The doctor was grieved very greatly, and walked the room and swore at his bad luck. Said he: "If it had been an ordinary bowl, I could replace it; in fact, it would be unnecessary to do so. But it was a piece of that beautiful set of imported ware, which can not be matched in the world."

Bleecker felt much sympathy for his friend, and tried to comfort him, but nothing he said seemed to improve matters. Finally he determined to try another plan, and said: "Doctor, when the horse threw you at Colonel Overton's, you promised" –

"Shut up! shut up! d— you!" said he, "don't you try to read moral lessons to me; the occasion requires heroic treatment." But the doctor was as brave as he was cultivated, and he went down to gather the fragments, and to make his confession to Mrs. Harding. Bleecker followed, and to the great delight of both the bowl was not broken. It fell into a drift of snow. Bleecker promised he would not tell what happened, but he could not keep it from the general, and soon all were enjoying the doctor's secret.

Soon after our army arrived at Nashville, General Forrest, with Buford's and Jackson's divisions, moved toward Murfreesboro to destroy the stockades and bridges along the Nashville and

Chattanooga Railroad, and prevent the enemy from receiving any assistance from that quarter. General Chalmers was, therefore, in command of the cavalry at Nashville. About 2 A.M. of December 15th, General Hood sent a courier with a note to General Chalmers, stating that the enemy would attack our lines that morning. We hurried over to Davidson's Landing, on the Charlotte pike, and found Rucker in a desperate fight with a greatly superior force. It was about the break of day, and the enemy was forming a column of cavalry to charge down the pike. This force was in addition to the troops fighting Rucker. General Chalmers quickly got a battery of smooth-bore guns in position, and, when the column of cavalry crossed the branch and started up the hill, grape shot were used with fearful effect. It was a terrible scene. Men and horses were killed, and others stumbled and fell over them. Our guns continued to fire, and the enemy on the right, shocked by the result, began to retreat. Rucker saw the opportunity, and, grasping a flag, raised it above his head and ordered a charge. He dashed along in front of his line, urging his men to push on. At the same time, General Chalmers with his escort charged them on the left, and within three minutes the enemy was on the run. We followed about a mile, until they reached their breast-works.

As we drove them back, we were joined by Colonel Mark Cockrell, mounted on a good horse. He rode in front, and called to our men to come on. The field belonged to Colonel Cockrell, and he was not less than seventy-five years of age, and had little, if any, use of his right arm. He held the reins in his mouth and his hat in his right hand. He was a picture, and his presence and bravery inspired our men to superhuman efforts. Unlike Dr. Henderson, he had taken no pledge, and he rode and swore in the very faces of the foes.

During that charge we lost many good men. All of the officers of the escort were severely wounded, and two were left in the enemy's lines and died in prison. In the meantime, General Hood's line had been driven back, and we found ourselves some three miles in advance of any other troops. We fell back to Davidson's Landing, and the gunboats on the river began to throw their big shells over us. They, however, did little damage. We could hear firing far to our rear, and the indications seemed that we were cut off. About 4 P.M., General Chalmers decided to fall back, and, if possible, join the main body of our retreating army. He ordered Bleecker ahead, with the escort company, as advance guard, with instructions to cross Walnut Ridge, and find the wagons which had been left on General Harding's race track. General Chalmers followed with Kelly's regiment, and Colonel Rucker with his brigade. Bleecker and the escort reached a point opposite Belle Meade, and, though the ridge was very steep, he succeeded in crossing, the men dismounting and leading their horses. General Chalmers, with Kelly's regiment, passed about a mile beyond and crossed. The weather was intensely cold, and snow and ice covered the ground. Bleecker reached the race track and found the wagons had been burned. He rode down near the pike, and saw Federal soldiers moving about in the yard of Belle Meade. Several of them had no guns. Some were on foot, others were mounted. He concluded it was a good opportunity, and moved the company around and behind the barn, where they formed for a charge. The boys went yelling and firing as they passed through the yard. The enemy, some two hundred in number, were surprised and ran. They had no idea there was a Confederate soldier in the neighborhood.

Bleecker pushed through the park, but, when near the creek, found a line of infantry behind a rock fence, and fell back. The enemy opened a hot fire, and, as the boys returned through the yard, the bullets were clipping the shrubbery, and striking the house. Nine of the enemy were killed or wounded, and some fifteen captured. As they rode back, Bleecker saw Miss Seline Harding standing on the stone arm of the front steps waving her handkerchief. The bullets were falling thick and fast about her, but she had no fear in her heart. She looked like a goddess. She was the gamest little human being in all the crowd. Bleecker passed and caught the handkerchief, and urged her to go into the house, but she would not, until the boys had disappeared behind the barn. They fell back across the pike, and awaited the coming of General Chalmers, who soon arrived. It was then dark, and

Bleecker explained the situation to the general, when he advanced a skirmish line and deceived the enemy as to his intentions.

From prisoners captured we found that General Wilson's cavalry had gone south on the Harding pike, and we then moved through the fields and woods toward our army, and succeeded in getting through, and by chance, found the left of General Hood's line, which had formed for a second defense. This was about daylight. Chalmers ordered General Rucker to guard the left flank, while he moved with his escort and Kelly's regiment toward Brentwood to find General Hood. As we passed along we came in sight of a column of Federal cavalry, which we charged and dispersed, then very soon caught up with General Cheatham's ambulances and some wagons, which we escorted to the Franklin pike. Arriving at Brentwood, we met General Hood, who quickly inquired, "What command is that?" Upon being told, he instructed General Chalmers to form his men across the pike and halt, and put in line every man going to the rear. We succeeded in getting about five hundred in line, when the stragglers began to crowd through, and finally all left us. General Hood was greatly distressed, and said: "They are the people, let them go. Now is the time for soldiers." Those men were barefooted and disheartened; the greatly superior numbers of the enemy had driven them back, and they were thoroughly demoralized. There was no occasion during the war that tried men more than that at Nashville. Ordinary soldiers will go forward and perform gallant deeds when the enemy is retreating, but it takes a hero to stand against overwhelming numbers advancing on him. Any soldier will laugh and cheer as he advances, but it takes a man to smile on a retreat.

While we were at Brentwood, General Rucker was attacked by a large force. Some of his men were driven back, leaving a gap in his line. He moved ahead with the Seventh Alabama to strike the enemy's flank, and placed them in position, then he rode a short distance to a point where he expected to find the Twelfth Tennessee, and found himself surrounded by a regiment of Federal cavalry. He at first thought they were his men, and asked for the colonel. As the commanding officer rode to meet him Rucker discovered he was a Federal, and drew his saber. The Federal officer did the same, and like game-cocks they began the battle. Rucker make a desperate rush at his antagonist, striking with all his power, and somehow dropped his saber, but instantly caught the Federal officer's arm and wrenched the saber from his hand and struck him a heavy blow with it. Very quickly he was surrounded, but with that energy, determination, and perhaps recklessness, which we had so often seen in Rucker, he tried to escape. He plunged the spurs into his horse, and forced his way, but he had gone but a short distance when the enemy began to shout, "Kill the man on the white horse," and hundreds of shots were fired at him. A man tried to cut him off, but Colonel Rucker struck him with the saber he had taken from the Federal colonel, and dismounted him. Just at that moment, however, a ball shattered his left arm above the elbow, and another killed his horse. Both fell, and the enemy rushed on him like wolves. They had no mercy for him, though he was almost unconscious from the fall. They pulled and hauled him around, swearing and calling him ugly names. He was finally moved to Nashville, where his arm was amputated. Colonel Rucker was promoted, and made a brigadier-general, but he was never able during the remainder of the war to assume command. He is now a citizen of Birmingham, Alabama.

By the night of December 16th, our army was in hasty retreat. The Federal forces under General Thomas numbered about fifty thousand infantry, one hundred and fifty pieces of artillery, and twelve thousand cavalry, while General Hood's force amounted to twenty-two thousand infantry, eighty pieces of artillery, and eighteen hundred cavalry. It does seem, therefore, that Hood made a noble resistance at Nashville, and why Thomas did not cut him off and capture the entire force before crossing the Tennessee river, is a matter for investigation. The wisdom of this campaign has been severely criticised. All night our troops trudged along toward Franklin. The ground was frozen, and many of the men barefooted, and scarcely any organization could be found. Had the situation been reversed, and Forrest in command of nine thousand cavalry, following the defeated twenty thousand men, not one of them would have escaped. The Federal cavalry in pursuit of Hood's army from Nashville was very poorly handled. In fact, the conduct of the officers, had they been Confederates, would have been regarded as criminal.

The morning of December 17th our troops were all on the south bank of the big Harpeth. General S.D. Lee with about four thousand infantry was in line on the hill south of Franklin to check the enemy's advance. General Buford joined us at Franklin, with Bell's and Lyon's brigades. The cavalry was all under the command of General Chalmers. Bell's brigade was skirmishing with the enemy across the river, and General Lee rode in that direction, and soon received a wound in the foot, and was compelled to give up the command to Major-General C.L. Stevenson. As soon as the straggling, foot-sore and starving men were out of reach we fell back toward Spring Hill. About six miles distant we halted again, and formed on the crest of a hill just south of a brick church. It was nearly night, very cold, and a mist or fog hung over every thing. The infantry continued the march, and Chalmers and Buford were left to resist the attack of nearly five times their number. Soon we saw the enemy's advance guard halt near the church. General Stevenson asked if they were our troops. General Chalmers answered, "No, they are Yankees," and before the brief conversation ended ten or twelve guns opened on us, and one among the first shots struck one of Walton's pieces full in the mouth, and knocked it off the carriage. In an instant the cavalry was on us, some firing their carbines, others using their sabers. It was a terrible mixing up of men and horses. The writer saw a Yankee slash General Buford twice over the shoulders with his saber, and he was paid for his daring by two bullets from General Chalmers' pistol. We were overpowered and driven back, but the infantry halted, and we formed again. The enemy, however, did not renew the attack that night. It was a dreadful night, the mud about a foot deep was frozen, but not sufficiently to bear the weight of our horses and the artillery.

We reached Spring Hill, and found that General Cheatham had thrown up temporary breast-works, and he remained there until the wagons and artillery were safely across the Duck river.

The enemy made two attacks upon us, but were easily repulsed. We crossed Duck river, and remained at Columbia the night of the 19th, when General Forrest reached us. General Hood immediately sent for him, and after discussing the situation, said he had great fear for the safety of the army. General Forrest replied that he would undertake to defend the rear of the army if he would give him Walthall and about four thousand infantry in addition to his cavalry force. General Hood promised to do so, and detailed Walthall's division of Stewart's corps for the service, but there were less than two thousand men in the division for duty, and fully a third of those barefooted. The wagons and whatever else was left of Hood's army moved south from Columbia early on the morning of the 19th, leaving General Forrest with the small infantry force and about three thousand cavalry to hold in check the advancing Federals. The enemy made no effort to cross the river that morning, but late in the afternoon began to shell the city of Columbia most furiously. General Forrest rode to the river bank under a flag of truce, and asked that the Federal commander come to the opposite shore. General Forrest assured him (General Hatch) that there was not a Confederate soldier in the town, but that there were some two thousand prisoners, some of them wounded, while others were sick and suffering from the severe cold. General Hatch then ordered the shelling to cease. General Forrest then proposed to exchange the prisoners for the same number of our men, and after two hours or so the answer came from General Thomas that he refused to exchange the prisoners, or to accept those Forrest had on parole. General Forrest said then to General Hatch that many of them were without proper clothing, and they would, therefore, most likely die from exposure, but the Federal officers would not accept them on parole. Perhaps when the final Judge shall call all men before the bar to answer for their actions, Thomas and Hatch will be met by the thousands of poor Federal prisoners who died from cold and wounds on that retreat.

Forrest remained at Columbia until the morning of the 22d, then fell back about three miles and occupied a most favorable position between two large hills near Lynnville. By this time,

Major-General Edward Cary Walthall

all our forces and the wagons were safely on the way to the south. There was desperate fighting between Lynnville and Pulaski, but the enemy never once broke our line. Walthall's men displayed great courage, as did also their commander. General Walthall was an inspiration. He was courtly and brave, and his tall, handsome form, splendid bearing, and fine, intelligent face will never be forgotten by the men of that army. His deeds will forever shed luster on the Confederate army and upon the American people. He was always ready, always prompt, and always wise. He never failed to accomplish what he was ordered to do, or in what he undertook on his own responsibility. He was the highest type of an American soldier and gentleman, and is to-day the ideal representative of the South in the United States Senate.

No man in the world ever had greater responsibilities resting upon him than did General Forrest on the retreat from Columbia, but he met them with great skill and cheerfulness. With a force of less than five thousand men, he was called to hold in check an army of fifty thousand. The writer does not believe that any other man on earth could have done this. Forrest represented in war what Cicero did in literature. He had a love for the right and a sincere respect for any demand for fairness. He was strong in character, profound in strategy, and forceful in battle. We will never see his like again.

We crossed the Tennessee river at Bainbridge on December the 27th, Chalmers' division being the last to cross, and moved quietly toward the prairie country for rest and food. There is nothing in the annals of war that will compare with the retreat from Nashville, particularly from Columbia to the Tennessee river, and the conduct of the men under Forrest will stand forever without a parallel.

CHAPTER TWENTY-FOUR

Reorganization of Forrest's Cavalry at Columbus, Miss. – The Surrender – General Forrest's Farewell Address – Tribute to General Grant

After reaching Corinth, the men who lived in Alabama, Tennessee, and Mississippi were furloughed for the purpose of getting fresh horses and better clothing. The Confederate Government, recognizing the great services of General Forrest, made him a lieutenant-general on February 28, 1865, and gave him command of all the cavalry in the Department of Alabama, Mississippi, and East Louisiana, and he immediately began to reorganize his forces. General Chalmers was given a division composed of three brigades of Mississippians, commanded by Brigadier-Generals Frank C. Armstrong, Wirt Adams, and P. B. Starke, numbering four thousand five hundred men. General Buford's division was made up of Alabama and Kentucky troops, while the division commanded by General W. H. Jackson comprised the Tennessee and Texas troops, about six thousand men, making a total of ten thousand five hundred men. Chalmers' division had camped at Columbus, Mississippi, for several weeks, but about the middle of March he was ordered to move to Selma with all possible haste to meet General Wilson, who had started in that direction with fifteen thousand troops. Adams' brigade was left at Columbus to guard the Mobile and Ohio Road. Jackson was ordered to Monte Vallo, Alabama, while Buford's division was not yet organized.

Forrest therefore went forward with about six thousand men to meet perhaps the best equipped cavalry force that had ever been organized up to that time. Wilson carried an immense wagon train, with a complete pontoon bridge, capable of spanning any river except the Mississippi. Besides, he had pack mules; also ample forage and other supplies. Wilson suddenly changed his direction toward Monte Vallo, and destroyed all the furnaces on the North and South Alabama Railroad. In the meantime, it began to rain, and all creeks and rivers were soon impassable to our forces. Wilson, appreciating the value of his boats, bridged the different streams, and threw overwhelming odds against our scattered forces and drove them off. It was impossible to concentrate our troops, because of impassable and swollen streams, the bridges having been all washed away. General Forrest could not communicate with General Chalmers until the morning of April the 1st, and by this time the enemy had possession of every favorable position. Forrest made an effort to reach Selma with sufficient force to defend the place, but was unable to do so, and there was fierce fighting for several days. When he realized that it would be impossible to head Wilson off, he moved to Marion, and then to Gainesville, Alabama. At the latter place, we heard of the surrender of General Lee, and in a few days heard that Mobile had fallen also. After a few days of further waiting, General Taylor surrendered the department, when all the proud hopes, lofty ambitions, long, weary marches, desperate battles, and anxiety for loved ones at home, found an end.

We remained at Gainesville until May the 9th, when the commissioner appointed by the United States Government (General E.S. Dennis) arrived, and began to parole our men. While we waited, the men became very restless, and were anxious to get home. They had suffered for several years without reward, except the consciousness of having made the grandest soldiers in all the world's history.

At the last reorganization, Bleecker was permanently assigned to the escort company, and was in command at the surrender. He was devoted to the boys, and the partings were with much regret and deep feelings. While they waited for the last act of the war, they amused themselves running horse and foot races. They were camped near the Tombigbee river, along the bank of which was a beautiful track of some six or eight hundred yards. Bleecker was very fleet-footed, and the escort company were willing to back him against all comers. He had never been beaten. Finally Buford's Kentucky brigade sent a man over to take the honors from him. It was a memorable occasion. The Kentuckians lined up on one side of the track, and Bleecker's friends on the other. One hundred yards were measured off, and they toed the line. Men bet their horses, saddles, spurs, pistols, and even their pocket knives. The word was given, and away they sped. Bleecker would rather have died than had the boys disappointed in him, and there was no occasion in his life when his pride was more at stake. They ran breast and breast for fifty yards or so, then Bleecker took the lead and won easily. It was the proudest moment of his life. Friends raised him off his feet and carried him above their heads. The Kentucky boys took their defeat heroically, but they lost every thing.

Before bidding good-bye to the soldiers, General Forrest issued a farewell address, which we give in full, and which illustrates his character:

> Headquarters Forrest's Cavalry Corps,
> Gainesville, Ala., May 9, 1865.
>
> *Soldiers* – By an agreement made between Lieutenant-General Taylor, commanding the department of Alabama, Mississippi, and East Louisiana; and Major-General Canby, commanding the United States forces, the troops of this department have been surrendered.
>
> I do not think it proper or necessary at this time to refer to the causes which have reduced us to this extremity; nor is it now a matter of material consequence to us how such results were brought about. That we are beaten, is a self-evident fact, and any further resistance on our part would be justly regarded as the very height of folly and rashness. The armies of Generals Lee and Johnson having surrendered, you are the last of all the troops of the Confederate States army, east of the Mississippi river, to lay down arms.
>
> The cause for which you have so long and so manfully struggled, and for which you have braved dangers, endured pri-

vations and sufferings, and made so many sacrifices, is today hopeless. The government which we sought to establish and perpetuate is at an end. Reason dictates and humanity demands that no more blood be shed. Fully realizing and feeling that such is the case, it is your duty and mine to lay down our arms, submit to the "powers that be," and to aid in restoring peace and establishing law and order throughout the land.

The terms upon which you were surrendered are favorable, and should be satisfactory and acceptable to all. They manifest a spirit of magnanimity and liberality on the part of the Federal authorities, which should be met on our part by a faithful compliance with all the stipulations and conditions therein expressed. As your commander, I sincerely hope that every officer and soldier of my command will cheerfully obey the orders given, and carry out in good faith all the terms of the cartel.

Those who neglect the terms, and refuse to be paroled, may assuredly expect, when arrested, to be sent North and imprisoned.

Let those who are absent from their commands, from whatever cause, report at once to this place, or to Jackson, Miss.; or if too remote from either, to the nearest United States post or garrison for parole.

Civil war, such as you have just passed through, naturally engenders feelings of animosity, hatred, and revenge. It is our duty to divest ourselves of all such feelings; and, as far as in our power to do so, to cultivate friendly feelings toward those with whom we have so long contended, and heretofore so widely, but honestly, differed. Neighborhood feuds, personal animosities, and private differences should be blotted out; and, when you return home, a manly, straightforward course of conduct will secure the respect even of your enemies. Whatever your responsibilities may be to government, to society, or to individuals, meet them like men. The attempt made to establish a separate and independent Confederation has failed; but the consciousness of having done your duty faithfully, and to the end, will, in some measure, repay for the hardships you have undergone.

In bidding you farewell, rest assured that you carry with you my best wishes for your future welfare and happiness. Without in any way referring to the merits of the cause in which we have been engaged, your courage and determination, as exhibited on many hard fought fields, have elicited the respect and admiration of friend and foe, and I now cheerfully and gratefully acknowledge my indebtedness to the officers and men of my command, whose zeal, fidelity, and unflinching bravery have been the great source of my past success in arms.

I have never, on the field of battle, sent you where I was unwilling to go myself; nor would I now advise you to a course which I felt myself unwilling to pursue. You have been good soldiers, you can be good citizens. Obey the laws, preserve your honor, and the government to which you have surrendered can afford to be and will be magnanimous.

N. B. Forrest, *Lieutenant-General.*

The effort had failed, and the Southern cause had gone down. It was the Titanic, political and social movement of the century. The principles must be consigned to time, but the effect upon the destinies of the country will be felt for a long period, and will finally redound to the benefit of our America.

The Confederate army had made a name for bravery and daring for the rank and file, and genius for the leaders, that will challenge the admiration of future generations, and establish a standard for emulation never to be excelled. In all the claims for distinction which may arise, there will come up the recollections of that proud and distinguished little army of half-starved, but heroic, soldiers, which stood for four years against the mighty hosts of men, resources, power, and money.

The official records of the United States Government show that there were enlisted on the Southern side during the entire war less than 600,000 men, while the Federal army numbered 2,872,304 men. Of the latter, 178,975 were Negroes. At the close of the war, the Confederates had 167,000 men in the field, while the North had 1,000,000 men in active service. The South, at no time during the war, had quite 300,000 men in the field, while her rivers and bays were packed with gun-boats, and 500 men of war guarded and closed her ports. When the future generations read the story, they will stand amazed. There were commanders on the Federal side whose greatest achievements consisted in destroying private property, burning churches and schoolhouses, and devastating the country; men who took pride in burning homes, and who cherished the opportunity to telegraph the government that "a crow passing over the line of my march must take his rations along or starve."

During Sherman's march through Georgia, his men hung old and defenseless people to make them tell where their valuables were. They took rings from the fingers of ladies and burned every thing which they could not carry away. This was desolation, not war. It was the wicked and savage hate he bore the Southern people, that spared neither age nor sex, nor condition, but like "Mephistopheles" gloated over the misery which he brought to helpless women and children, that prompted and approved such acts. They could not whip the Southern soldier in battle, but could destroy their homes and starve their families.

Nearly the third of a century has passed away. The passions which the unhappy conflict inflamed have had time to cool. The prejudices engendered have been abated. The many asperities incident have been mitigated, and the prejudices, wrongs and hates of the day are forgotten or forgiven. The South has arisen from her ashes and desolation. Her valleys are smiling, her granaries are full, her cities progressive and prosperous, her homes happy. The same people who saw her trampled in the dust by an invading foe, and who fought violently to defend her, have transformed her into a thing of beauty. Former foes are friends, peace has returned, and the South is following her grand destiny, but the heart of the Southern soldier is unchanged as to the conduct of some of the Northern generals, and it will remain unchanged.

For Butler, who made war on the ladies in New Orleans, who disgraced the name of soldier by his conduct and brutality, there is a feeling of condemnation.

But there was one Federal general whose name lends luster to the American soldier and to the American citizen, who is respected and revered by every fair minded man, who understood the prowess of the Southern soldier, and who removed from the South the sting of defeat by the magic touch of his magnanimity in dealing with the vanquished. Around the name of U.S. Grant can cluster the hopes of a national feeling of a reunited and indissoluble union of all the States. Grant was the genius of the war on the Federal side. He realized that he must overpower the South, and therefore concentrated his forces for final struggle, but he never made war on defenseless women and old men. He knew the value of a recruit to the South, and therefore declined the exchange of prisoners. He crushed the Confederacy with superior numbers, but he paroled and trusted the Confederate. He knew that if he put the Southern soldier on his honor he would make a good citizen, but that if the leaders were imprisoned, the Southern people would become a nation of "bushwhackers," and he told President Johnson that the army of the United States would be used to carry out the terms and conditions of General Lee's surrender, if necessary. By that act he bound to him with hooks of steel the Southern hearts, which his magnanimity won at Appomattox.

PART III.

"LAGNIAPPE"

I.
King Philip

After the war, General Forrest, with his wife and son, Captain Billy Forrest, went to live on his farm in Coahoma county, Mississippi. It was the middle of May, and too late to plant cotton, but they raised an enormous crop of corn. At that time, the "Mississippi Delta" was known as the "Bottom," and was invariably referred to as such. The country was sparsely settled, and in many cases farm-houses were five and six miles apart, and the general's place was no exception. Less than ten per cent of the country had been cleared; therefore the timber and cane made it a wilderness. There was no occasion for Federal troops in that country, because the population was too small to require watching, and there had been none there until about the first of August.

The affairs at the Forrest home were quiet and undisturbed. Both the general and Captain Billy were busily engaged restoring the fences and repairing and rebuilding the houses. The general had erected a saw-mill, to which he gave his personal attention. In fact, he performed the work of what was styled "a full hand," besides managing and looking after the laborers, his old slaves, to whom he was then paying wages. They were devoted to "Mars. Bedford." Captain Billy was detailed to drive the ox team, which was used to haul logs to the mill. There was a luxuriant Bermuda grass lot in front of the house, where the horses grazed during the day. General Forrest had given instructions that King Philip should never be saddled again. Like the Negroes, he was set free. The general appreciated his great services during the war, and decided to emancipate him. Jerry, the general's body servant, and Pat, an Irishman who served him as orderly while in the service, were employed about the house and lot. Fields of beautiful corn surrounded the house, and the rustling of the blades of fodder, together with the graceful bending of the tassels as they yielded to the soft summer breezes, gave the place an air of quiet and domestic life, very different from that which the owner and his family and servants and horses had been accustomed to for several years past.

It was a warm August morning, about 10 o'clock. King Philip and the other horses were grazing in the lot, when a company of Federal cavalry rode up to the "big gate" and halted. They were searching for government cotton, and hearing that the rebel General Forrest lived there, desired to take advantage of the opportunity and see him. King Philip was the same character of horse that Forrest was man, and seemed to have been made for just such service as he had seen the past two years. His education had been well attended to during that time. He had never come in view of a company of Federals without having to rush at them with all his speed and energy. No doubt it was with him instinctively a thing which he had no power to resist, and, perhaps, no disposition to avoid. The Federal captain and his company, ignorant of the character of King Philip, and therefore of impending danger, and confident of their ability to defend themselves, opened the gate and rode in. King Philip had by that time, doubtless, forgotten the horrors of war, as he nipped the fresh young grass, and did not discover the presence of the blue coats until they had entered the lot. He heard the tramp of the horses and looked up, and the old passion, born of education and hard experience, took possession of him. With head and tail in the air, he rushed at the company with his old-time energy, nor did he halt until every man and horse had been driven from the lot. He kicked and fought like a tiger. After the gate had been closed, he galloped along the fence-row, neighing and shaking his head defiantly. Jerry, hearing the noise and seeing the commotion, ran down to the gate and heard dreadful threats against Philip. One of the men, who was severely hurt by a kick, swore he would kill him; but Jerry grasped a fence-rail, and announced that he would defend Philip with his life; and that was the situation when General Forrest and Captain Billy returned home for dinner.

The officer explained the occurrence to the general, who, after King Philip had been put in the stable, invited the whole company in for dinner and rest. Jerry said: "'Twus not King Philip's fault; dem Yankees opened the gate and rid in bedout sayin nuthin to nobody."

After all had been seated on the gallery and had laughed over the affair, the Federal captain said: "General, I can now account for your success; your Negroes fight for you and your horses fight for you."

The general soon after had occasion to go to Memphis on business, and told the story to some of his friends. At that time, there were a number of sick and wounded men in the city who needed means and attention. It was at once suggested that an entertainment be gotten up for their benefit, and that old Philip be exhibited as one of the features. The general consented, and returned home and gave instructions to Pat and Jerry to put him in nice condition. They began giving him extra attention, and feeding him quantities of green corn. Early one morning, not long after the general's return from Memphis, Jerry knocked at his door, and between sobs and lamentations told him that King Philip was dead. The general hurriedly dressed and went to the stable, and found Pat kneeling down and caressing his neck and shedding bitter tears. The general himself wiped away a tear, and expressed great sorrow. Pat, believing that the general would take his death very seriously, thought to relieve him of his sorrow, and said: "Gineral, he is dead, King Philip is dead! But, sir, I want you to look at the good fat I put on him before he died." King Philip died with the colic, and, of course, was badly swollen, but Pat wanted the general to think it was fat.

II.
Anecdote of General Forrest

Not long after the war, General Forrest and his son, Captain Billy, went to New York. It was the first time either of them ever saw the great city. At that time, the "St. Nicholas" was the popular hotel for Southern people, and it was at that hostelry they stopped. They arrived about night, and after an early breakfast the following morning, concluded to go out and see the city. The rotunda of the St. Nicholas was on a level with the street. They walked to the front and stopped to get their bearings. There was a great crowd of people in front of the hotel, which rapidly grew larger after they halted. The general wore a grey suit and a broad brimmed light colored felt hat. He was at all times a conspicuous figure, but his friends at home were accustomed to him, therefore did not appreciate his distinguished appearance as strangers did. The papers announced that he was in the city, and there was wide-spread curiosity to see him. He was ignorant of the cause that drew the crowd together, and, having heard that Broadway was a great thoroughfare, supposed it was a natural condition.

Finally, he heard a person say, "That's him. That's the rebel, General Forrest," and he made his way out, and, with Captain Billy, walked up the street. The crowd followed, and was augmented at every corner. Those in front were pressed by those following, until finally hundreds of them were blocking up the street and sidewalk looking at the big rebel. The general grew restless and worried over the situation, but, as was invariably the case, he was equal to the occasion. He lifted his big white hat high above his head, and cried out with a voice that had never failed to produce consternation: "Get out of my way, G–d d— you." The effect was instantaneous. Those in the rear were knocked down and run over by those in front, and the stampede lasted for several minutes during which time the general and Captain Billy went into a cross street and escaped further intrusion.

The afternoon papers mentioned the circumstances, and the morning papers were full of it. Forrest was discussed by every tongue. The following morning he sat on the side of his bed, had just pulled on his boots, and was coursing his fingers through his hair, a very common habit with him. (The writer has often seen him when his long, iron-gray hair stood up, "like quills upon the fretful porcupine.") He had not yet removed his night-shirt, when some one knocked at his door. Captain Billy occupied an adjoining room with a door opening into the general's, and went to the outer door to answer the knock. He was astonished to find a lady there. She was a typical New England old maid; tall, angular, and thin; her hair was dark and pasted tightly over her high forehead; thin lips, compressed mouth, and a well distinguished jaw. She carried a Bible in one hand, and an umbrella in the other. She pushed Captain Billy aside, and advancing, addressing the General, asked: "Are you the Rebel General Forrest? And is it true that you murdered those dear colored people at Fort Pillow? Tell me, sir; I want no evasive answer!"

The writer does not think that slang is good taste, or good sense, but he feels that, in this instance, a slang phrase conveys the ideal plainly: "She got it in the neck."

The general rose up from his bed to his full height, his hair standing on end, and said: "Yes, madam; I killed the men and women, and ate the babies for breakfast."

The old maid ran screaming down the hall-way and into the street.

III.
Carpet Baggers

After the war had ended, the South was overrun by a class called "Carpet Baggers." They were as a general and almost universal thing the scum of the earth. Men who, except in a few instances, had no idea of right, honesty, gentility, or decency, and knew no such law or motto. They came South to fire the heart of the newly-emancipated Negro, and organize a political party, by which they could obtain official control of the different States. They were not representatives of any class in the North, nor anywhere else on God's green earth, but were to the North what the bench-leg fice (of which no female was ever known) is to the canine tribe. They organized secret societies, and administered the most terrible oaths to the Negroes. They promised to give each voter forty acres of land and a mule, if he would vote properly. The forty acres and the mule did not materialize, however, and the Negroes began to complain. In the meantime every scoundrel of them had ridden into office on the Negro votes. Finally it was necessary to made new promises, or else the Negroes would withdraw their support. State officers and a legislature had to be elected, so the Carpet Baggers gave it out that the Republicans had affairs working nicely, and if reelected they would pass a bill with provisions in it for the colored man. The poor, ignorant things spent a month drilling, and moving from one place to another, sitting up at nights, and taking new oaths "to 'spise the White folks." After the election, hundreds of them wasted their time hanging around the town, with sacks and cotton baskets, waiting for the "provisions," and after they were entirely without food, went among the White people and asked for bread. No Carpet Bagger ever felt sympathy enough for a Negro to help him. Those rascals passed a law that all Negroes who were living together as man and wife, must obtain license and be married. It will be understood that all the clerks of the courts were Carpet Baggers, and they in this way got thousands of dollars from the deluded and unfortunate Negroes. Those who had been living together years and years, and who had grand-children, were required to pay two dollars for license, and then pay a magistrate one dollar to perform the ceremony.

They robbed and imposed upon the Negroes, but the poor things, like an ox, would suffer in silence. "'T would not do to tell de White folks."

There were several species of Carpet Baggers, as is the case with the monkey family: gray monkeys, red monkeys, big monkeys, little monkeys, ring-tail monkeys, etc. Different grades of Carpet Baggers performed different duties. There was an "Old He One" in every county, whom the little ring-tails reported to, and received orders from. The little ring-tails went over the county selling pegs, some were painted red, and others white. They were sold in sets of four. The red ones were sold at ten dollars, and the white ones at five dollars per set. The purchaser was told that he could use the pegs for staking off ground. The red pegs were sold to stake off eighty acres, and the white pegs good for forty acres of land. A prominent farmer in Madison county, Mississippi, Colonel Jefferson Love, in riding over his place, noticed the pegs, and inquired who put them there. One of his old slaves said: "I did, sir. Dey is de pegs whur Gineral Grant sarnt me; dey marks my ground whur de guvernment dun gin me." The gentleman tried to explain to the old man that he had been duped, but it did no good. Finally, like the man in the fable, when he found that kind words and grass had no effect upon the boy, he tried rocks. The rocks brought him down. The old Negro returned the pegs to the ring-tail and demanded his money, but he died without getting it. The ring-tail told him that if he would wait until fall, the pegs would be good.

When the Negroes would begin to grow callous, after repeated deceptions, the Carpet Bagger would tell them General Grant sent word, "They must do so and so," and immediately every one was in line. If one of the ring-tails needed money, all that was necessary to raise it was the order of General Grant.

These are facts which people living in the North will not readily believe, but they are true; and when believed and recognized to have been the true condition of affairs in the South during what was known as the Reconstruction period, the Northern people then must admit that the White people of the South were more tolerant and the Negroes more gullible and more grossly deceived and imposed upon by their pretended friends, the said Carpet Baggers, than ever any people were on earth.

IV.
"Nashville Pintincy"

A Negro boy employed as butler by a prominent family on Vance street, Memphis, requested the young lady of the house to write for him a letter to his sweet-heart. She sat down to her escritoire to comply, and asked: "How shall I begin it, John?" "Oh, jes like de young gemmins start dar letters to you, Miss R.," he answered. Miss R. assured John that there was no stereotyped style in opening correspondence with her. She wrote the letter, however, which she read to John, and asked if it was satisfactory.

"Yes'um, I suppose it mout do, but 'scuse me, Miss R., if I defer a subgestion. I ud like to put a little bit mo' in dar like dis:

> De rose am red, and de vylets blue,
> De pinks am preaty, an', an', so is you.

After having acted upon John's "subgestion," she asked if that was all.

John scratched his woolly head a moment, and then said: "Miss R., dar am one more thing what oughten to go in dar. Dis: 'I hopes dat you will 'scuse de pore mizzerable writin' and de bad spellin'.'"

The letter finally satisfied John, and Miss R. asked how it should be addressed.

Said he: "To Miss Mary Malone, care Nashville Pintincy."

"Why, John, she is not in the penitentiary, is she?"

"Yes'um, oh, yes 'um," said he.

"Well," said Miss R., "how on earth came she there?"

"Oh, nuthin' much; she gist steal some, and kit kotched, dat wuz all."

V.
Anecdote of Hon. Chas. Ready

During the war, wherever the Federals got a foothold, they arrested and imprisoned the most prominent people. No reason or excuse was given for the action, and it was well known to be a part of a system to humiliate and punish men who were too old to go in the service. Prominent among a number of distinguished gentlemen who were placed in the penitentiary at Nashville was the Hon. Charles Ready, of Murfreesboro, Tennessee. Judge Ready was a lawyer of conspicuous ability and a citizen of the highest character. He was the friend of the poor and defenseless and a devoted husband and father. No man stood higher in the esteem of his neighbors than he. While, in the penitentiary, he met a Negro, who had been confined a number of years, and was doing duty as a "trusty." The Negro was named Dan, and was very polite and attentive to the judge. He polished his shoes and looked after his comfort generally.

    The judge was finally released and returned to his home at Murfreesboro. After the war, Dan, having served out his time, made straight for Murfreesboro. He had a very good understanding of human nature, and of a Southern gentleman in particular. He reached the judge's home during his absence, and was told by the servants to go off, but he remained in the vicinity until the judge returned. The judge was glad to see Dan, and gave instructions to the servants to treat him kindly. Mrs. Ready gave him a suit of good clothes, hat, and shoes, and Dan realized that he was in clover. The crumbs which he had cast on the waters had returned to him a thousand-fold. The servants turned up their noses at Dan, but it made no difference to him. He knew that he would be provided for. He was very fond of talking to the judge and Mrs. Ready, and often sat on the steps while they enjoyed their big rockers on the broad gallery, in the summer afternoons. Dan dated all his good fortune from the time he and the judge met in the penitentiary, and this was his theme on the afternoons referred to. He would laugh and tell Mrs. Ready "how me and judge used to do when we wus in the pinitinchery together." Mrs. Ready was a lady of cultivation and an unusually keen perception of things, and would laugh and encourage Dan to go on, but the judge was not so reminiscently inclined.

    During Dan's visit, on one occasion, the judge had been employed in a criminal case, which demanded the best attention. He gave the most earnest consideration to it, and secured a verdict of acquittal for his client. He was a liberal, impulsive, kind, and generous man. He was conscious of having given his best energy to the case, and wanted to cap off the occasion by inviting a number of his friends and brother lawyers to dine with him. Mrs. Ready was always pleased to entertain his friends, and on this occasion made extra preparation. After dinner, the gentlemen repaired to the gallery to enjoy a fine brand of cigars which were handed them. Soon Dan made his appearance on the steps and began to tell "what me and the judge used to do when we wus in the pinitinchery together." There was a gentleman in the party that had but recently moved to Murfreesboro from the North, and had never heard of the imprisonment of gentlemen for political reasons. He heard Dan's tale, and noticed that no contradiction of his statement was made. Finally, he asked what it meant.

"Why," said one of the gentlemen, "are you not aware that the judge served a term in the penitentiary, and that the Negro was in at the same time?"

The newcomer had never heard of it, and, indeed, few Northern men of the present day know how prominent Southerners were made to suffer during the war.

VI.
The Negroes

Having written with the sole purpose of leaving to my posterity and to such others as may feel sufficient interest in a simple, but true, narrative of the stirring events of 1861 to 1865 to read it, and having been prevailed on to publish the story in a durable form, I feel that I should leave my self-imposed task (which is more a labor of love than a task) incomplete, did I fail or neglect to bear testimony to the fidelity of the Negroes to their masters' families during those dark and dreadful days. Slavery existed in the Southern States alone, and prior to the war there had been more than one insurrectionary movement among the slaves, and one (that of Southampton, Virginia, led by Nat Turner) had cost much innocent blood and created a world-wide sensation. All these insurrections and attempted insurrections were believed to have been incited by two agencies; first, evil disposed, envious, or intermeddling incendiaries from the free States, and second, a burning desire upon the part of some of the more intelligent Negroes to throw off the yoke of slavery and be free. It is needless to recall the horrors of those outbreaks, but they occurred, and never without involving the shedding of human blood and the sacrifice of life.

There may have been instances in which malice, wrought up by harsh and cruel treatment of slaves by heartless and brutish owners, were among the incitements, but, as a rule, slave owners and especially those who were kind, considerate, and just to their slaves, were highly respected and sincerely beloved by the latter, and no stronger proof of this fact could be desired than was afforded by the conduct of the slaves generally during the late war. For months and even years, the families of the South were almost wholly at the mercy of the Blacks. There was many a night on which ladies and children were the only Whites on a Southern plantation, or at a Southern home. There were weeks and months of such nights, and yet from the beginning to the end of the war, no such thing as an insurrectionary movement was known or heard of, nor the use of any incendiary or insulting language whatever charged, reported, or hinted against the Negroes. True, a number of them left their owners and their homes, or were carried or enticed away, and many of the men who went enlisted in the Federal army. But, on the other hand, a majority of them remained at home, and actually hid themselves and the stock of their owners whenever they heard the startling cry, "Yankees coming." This is positively true. I could cite instances and name parties and places were it necessary. Not only did a large majority of the Negroes remain at their homes, but they took care of the property and families of their owners, raised crops, and did all other customary and necessary work, just as they had done before the war, when owners and overseers watched over them. These are facts that flatly contradict and give the lie direct to the numerous oft-repeated assertions of Abolitionists (slanders on the Negroes), that they hated the Whites of the South, and only worked for and obeyed them because they were compelled to do so. Not only did a very large majority of the Negroes remain at home during the war, but after they were made free as a result of the war, and by National and State action, many still remained with their former owners and worked for them for regular wages or "on shares," and not a few are still doing so.

These are facts, and no matter what may be the outcome of the developments of the future, as a race, the Negroes, by their conduct and their fidelity in times and under circumstances that might well have been supposed, would and did put their allegiance and fidelity to the severest test, earned and entitled themselves to the kind consideration, the friendship, and love of the Whites. True, after the war had ended and they became free, their ignorance was imposed upon, and many of them allowed themselves to be duped and misled into a feeling of distrust and a course of antagonism to their former owners, and the Whites of the South generally, which came very near causing a rupture that must or might have resulted in the destruction of all confidences, the severance of all ties, and creating a permanent animosity among the races. I do not envy the men – the fiends – who could take advantage of the ignorant Blacks to turn them against the Whites, expose them to the possible dangers and evils of a bloody race conflict. Such men are too mean to live, and they are unfit to die.

Fortunately, the Negroes discovered the cloven foot of the marplot in time to avert it and when they withdrew their allegiance, the Carpet Bagger "left the country for the country's good," and perhaps their own safety (I do not quote literally, because it was not their country). They came for spoils, did all the meanness they could, duped and cheated those poor people who had trusted them, and when the "spoils" ceased to flow into their carpet bags, they returned whence they came, bitter in their feelings, because of the disappointment, then posed in the North as martyrs, and scattered falsehoods against the Southern people. I never knew of but one instance where one carried back a Negro wife. A person who served as sheriff of Yazoo county, Mississippi, took unto himself a Negro woman for a wife, and was married by a Negro preacher. He was afterward State senator. The writer knew them both, and will not hesitate to say the woman was superior to the man.

We do not denominate all Northern men who came South soon after the war and since that time as Carpet Baggers. Those we speak of were an entirely different set, and were a worse and more bitter curse to the Southern States, and to the people of the South, both White and Black, than was the four years of war, of which they were the degraded and unprincipled stragglers and scum. Those persons were always in the rear, and by them most of the thieving and other meanness was done. Nor do I hesitate to say that the better and more intelligent class of Negroes were by far the superiors of this despicable and unprincipled element.

After the Carpet Baggers had hied them away, the Negroes and the Whites got along without trouble, and they are getting along harmoniously to this day; and, except a few of the most restless and improvident, who would never be content to remain permanently any where, they are doing well, and conducting themselves well. And when I recall to mind how they conducted themselves during the war, and how faithful they were, my earnest hope and prayer is that they may continue to improve and that no discord may ever disturb the relations which now exist between the races in the South.

www.ingramcontent.com/pod-product-compliance
Lightning Source LLC
Chambersburg PA
CBHW071657090426
42738CB00009B/1567